S0-AHR-435

781.62009 McNeil v.1
Southern folk ballads
30519002607540

Southern Folk
Ballads

AMERICAN
FOLKLORE
SERIES

Southern Folk Ballads

Volume One

Compiled and edited by
W. K. McNeil

This Volume Is A Part Of
The American Folklore Series
W.K. McNeil, General Editor

August House / Little Rock
PUBLISHERS

PROPERTY OF
HIGH POINT PUBLIC LIBRARY
HIGH POINT, NORTH CAROLINA

Copyright 1987 by W. K. McNeil
All rights reserved. This book, or parts thereof,
may not be reproduced in any form without permission.
Published 1987 by August House, Inc.,
P.O. Box 3223, Little Rock, Arkansas,
501-663-7300.

Printed in the United States of America
10 9 8 7 6 5 4 3 2 1

LIBRARY OF CONGRESS CATALOGING-IN-PUBLICATION DATA

Southern folk ballads.
(The American folklore series)
Unacc. melodies.
Each melody is followed by
words printed as text and commentary.
Includes indexes.
"Biblio-discography": p. 167
1. Folk music—Southern States.
2. Ballads, English—Southern States.
I. McNeil, W. K. II. Series.
M1629.6.S7S68   1987   87-751904
ISBN 0-87483-038-9 (alk. paper)
ISBN 0-87483-039-7 (pbk.)

First Edition, 1987

Cover design by Communication Graphics
Cover photograph from Collections
of the Library of Congress
Production artwork by Ira L. Hocut
Typography by Arrow Connection, Pollock Pines, CA
Musical notation by Jan Barger
Design direction by Ted Parkhurst
Project direction by Liz Parkhurst

This book is printed on archival-quality paper which meets the
guidelines for performance and durability of the Committee on
Production Guidelines for Book Longevity of the Council on
Library Resources.

8706899

For Noble Cowden and to the memory of Almeda Riddle,
Southern folk ballad singers par excellence

8703393

Guide to reading musical notation

(1) All ballads are transcribed exactly as performed at the time of collection, even though there may be some irregularities in time, rhythm and notation.

(2) Time signatures enclosed in parentheses indicate that there will be variations from the stated time within the ballad. (For instance, the time signature for "The Broken-Hearted Boy" in the section "Ballads of Unfaithful Lovers" is listed as 4/4, even though measure 2 has 4 1/4 beats and measure 7 has 3 3/4 beats.)

(3) A short bar under a note indicates that that note is to be played or sung with special emphasis.

(4) In most cases, the melody line for a single verse is listed, although in cases where the melody differs from one stanza to another, the melody is listed either for the entire ballad or for the first stanza and the variant stanza.

Contents

Acknowledgments

Anyone with experience in book publishing knows that an author or editor is greatly relieved when his manuscript is completed. The editor of the present work is no exception to this general rule. Yet my delight at having finished this volume is no greater than my desire to acknowledge the help of those individuals without whom this book could not have been produced. They include Barry Jean Ancelet, Drew Beisswenger, Richard Blaustein, George W. Boswell, Dan Brackin, Thomas G. Burton, Kay L. Cothran, Frank de Caro, Dianne Dugaw, Burt Feintuch, Bill Ferris, George Foss, Bobby Fulcher, Ellen Garrison, Byrd Gibbens, Robert Halli, Don Hatley, Julie Henigan, Charles W. Joyner, Joyce Lamont, Bill Lightfoot, Ormond Loomis, Kip Lornell, Brenda McCallum, Bob McCarl, Tom McGowan, Roddy Moore, Dan Patterson, Dee Patterson, George Reinecke, Peter Roller, Sharon Sarthou, Mercedes Steely, John O. West, and Charles K. Wolfe. They were all gracious with their time and knowledge and much of what is worthwhile here is a result of their altruism. None of these people should be held accountable for any interpretations or errors found here; for those I claim sole responsibility.

W.K. McNeil
THE OZARK FOLK CENTER
MOUNTAIN VIEW, ARKANSAS

Introduction

This collection of ballads was mostly recorded since 1955 in the southern United States. Some are widely popular while others are known only in a relatively small area. A few originated in the South but most did not; instead they had their beginnings in various places ranging from the Old World to the commercial popular music industry of nineteenth- and twentieth-century America. They range in age from the early fifteenth century to the late 1920s. These certainly aren't the only ballads known in the South or necessarily even the most popular examples, although several of them would be found in any such listing. All of the ballads presented here are known in the South and, to that extent, they are representative Southern ballads although they are, in most cases, not unique to the region. Each song given here has been maintained by oral tradition and is thus an example of a folk ballad.

Several of these songs are taken from my own fieldwork, but most come from other collections and archives. I cannot claim that the informants whose contributions fill these pages were chosen by any design on my part. They just happened to have appropriate material that could be made immediately available to me. The method may seem somewhat haphazard but, because songs were sought from persons currently or recently doing ballad collecting in each state, the present selection does indicate to a considerable extent those areas where contemporary folksong fieldwork in the South has been concentrated. Evidently, my compilation is to a large degree dependent on the willingness of other collectors to share items with me and, although those people are credited in the acknowledgments, their unselfishness deserves mention here as well.

Obviously, many other volumes of Southern folk ballads could be compiled for not only can these materials be found in most communities in the South but folklorists, both amateur and professional, have spent many decades collecting ballads. Indeed, ballads may be the most frequently studied aspect of Southern folklore. This book, then, should be seen as an introductory rather than definitive work. In one respect, however, it is unique, namely in its attention to the entire South. Most ballad collections deal with one state or the entire nation or with a relatively small specific region like the Ozarks. There have even been collectors who did fieldwork in the entire South and there have been volumes dealing with ballads and folksongs of the western United States and New England, but, to my knowledge, no published collections dealing with the entire South. There is a book titled *Folksongs of the South* but it deals solely with West Virginia songs.

A number of terms used in this volume may be unfamiliar or confusing to many readers. First is the word *folklore,* which in popular usage is generally reserved for anything that is quaint or odd. That is not the exact meaning of the word, however, and not the one used in this book. Here, folklore refers to material that is passed on orally and, usually, informally; is traditional; undergoes change over space and time, creating variants and versions; is usually anonymous in the sense that most bearers of folklore are not concerned with the original creator; and finally, folklore is usually formulaic.[1]

Another definition essential for present purposes is *the South.* That is easily answered, for it refers to the states of Alabama, Arkansas, Florida, Georgia, Kentucky, Louisiana, Mississippi, North Carolina, South Carolina, Tennessee, Texas, and Virginia. In other words, the South is interpreted here as most of the states represented in the Confederacy during the Civil War. Admittedly, the Confederacy was a political rather than a cultural entity but these states do have a certain cultural and social unity although they definitely are not homogeneous. Moreover, these are the states often referred to when one speaks of "the South." Thus, logic is on the side of this particular drawing of the boundaries.[2]

A final term that must be defined is *ballad,* and to do so necessitates brief discussion of another word, *folksong.* Folklorists use the term *folksong* in two ways: as a generic word applied to all songs passed on by folksingers and as a means of distinguishing between lyric and narrative songs. *Ballad* is the term applied to folksongs that tell a story while folksong is reserved for those numbers that do not contain a narrative. But how much narrative does a song need to become a ballad? A song such as "I Can't Stay Here By Myself" which is made up entirely of "floating verses" (that is, verses found in numerous songs and seemingly fitting all equally well) would probably not be mistaken for a ballad even by novice folksong specialists. As the following lyrics make evident, it simply doesn't tell a connected narrative; it does suggest some story but never goes beyond the hint.

> *Oh, I wish I was a little bird,*
> *I'd fly through the top of a tree,*
> *I'd fly and sing a sad little song,*
> *I can't stay here by myself.*
>
> *I can't stay here by myself,*
> *I can't stay here by myself.*
> *I'd fly and sing a sad little song,*
> *I can't stay here by myself.*

Once I had plenty money,
My friends all around me would stand.
Now my pockets are empty
And I have not a friend in the land.

Farewell, farewell corn whiskey,
Farewell peach brandy too.
You've robbed my pockets of silver
And I have no use for you.

Oh, I wish I was a little fish,
I'd swim to the bottom of the sea.
I'd swim and sing a sad little song,
I can't stay here by myself.[3]

Likewise, it seems doubtful that any specialist would classify the number known variously as "The Creole Girl" or "The Lake of Pontchartrain" as anything other than a ballad:

It was on one Friday morning
I bid New Orleans adieu.
I made my way to Jackson
Where I was supposed to go.
Mid swamps and alligators
I made my weary way.
It was there I met that Creole girl
On the lake of Pontchartrain.

I said unto that Creole girl,
"My money to me is no good.
If it wasn't for the alligators
I'd sleep out in the woods."
"Oh, welcome, welcome stranger
Although our home is plain
We'll never turn a stranger down
On the lake of Pontchartrain."

She took me to her Mother's house
She treated me quite well.
Her hair in golden ringlets
Hung down [sic] her shoulders fell.
I tried to win her beauty
But I found it all in vain
To win the beauty of the Creole girl
On the lake of Pontchartrain.

> I asked her if she'd marry me.
> She said it could not be.
> That you have a lover
> And he was far off at sea.
> "Oh, yes, you have a lover
> And true you shall remain
> Until he returns to you again
> On the lake of Pontchartrain."
>
> I said unto that Creole girl,
> "Your face I shall see no more
> I'll never forget the kindness
> Or the cottage by the shore.
> When the moving sun shall circle
> And sparkling drinks I'll drink.
> I'll drink success to that Creole girl
> On the lake of Pontchartrain."[4]

There are, however, many other songs that are not so obviously in one camp or the other. For example, consider the following songs (respectively, "Miss, I Have a Very Fine Horse," "My Father Was a Spanish Merchant," and "Waggoner's Lad"):

> "Miss, I have a very fine horse
> That stands in yonder stall,
> That you may have at your command
> If you will be my bride, bride, bride,
> If you will be my bride."
>
> "Sir, I see your very fine horse
> That stands in yonder stall,
> But he knows his master will get drunk
> And's afraid that he will learn, learn, learn,
> And's afraid that he will learn."
>
> "Miss, I have a very fine house
> That's been newly rectified,
> That you may have at your command
> If you will be my bride, bride, bride,
> If you will be my bride."
>
> "Sir, I see your very fine house
> And also very fine yard
> But who's to stay with me at night
> When you are gambling and playing cards, cards,
> Gambling and playing cards?"
>
> "Miss, I never do that way
> I never thought it right
> But if you'll consent to marry me
> I'll not stay out one night, night, night,
> I'll not stay out one night."

"Sir, I know what that is for
It's just to take me in
And when you find the promise is true
You'll gamble and drink again, 'gain, 'gain,
You'll gamble and drink again!"

"Miss, I find you a very hard case
Perhaps too hard to please,
And some cold night when you are alone
I hope to my soul you'll freeze, freeze, freeze,
I hope to my soul you'll freeze."[5]

My father was a Spanish merchant
And before he went to sea,
He told me to be sure and answer,
"No," to all you said to me.
"No, sir! No, sir! No, sir! No!"

"If when walking in the garden
Plucking flowers all wet with dew
Tell me, would you be offended
If I walk and talk with you?"
"No, sir! No, sir! No, sir! No!"

"If I told you that I loved you
And would ask you to be mine
Tell me now, my pretty maiden,
Would you then my heart decline?"
"No, sir! No, sir! No, sir! No!"[6]

I am a poor girl, my fortune is sad
I've always been courted by a wagonner's lad,
He courted me gaily, by night and by day
And now he is loaded and going away.

Your horses are hungry, go feed them some hay.
Come sit down here by me as long as you stay.
My horses ain't hungry, they won't eat your hay,
So fare you well, darling, I'll be on my way.

Your wagon needs greasing, your whip needs to mend.
Come sit down here by me as long as you can.
My wagon is greasy, my whip's in my hand,
So fare you well darling, I'll no longer stand.[7]

Most folksong specialists would probably not classify either of the first two tunes here as a ballad but the third one is often so categorized. Yet, even the most superficial observer would likely say that the first song contains more of a story than the last one does. That being the case, why would it not be called a ballad? The answer is that most folksong specialists have followed the lead of the eighteenth-century poet William Shenstone who referred to ballads as those songs in which action predominates over sentiment.[8] In actual practice, though, classification often proves to be arbitrary. Thus, Celestin P. Cambiaire categorized a version of "Waggoner's Lad" as a ballad while the editors of the *Frank C. Brown Collection of North Carolina Folklore* present it as a folksong.[9]

In the South, as elsewhere in the United States, three types of ballads are known: Child ballads, broadside ballads, and native American ballads. Child ballads are not so called because they are for or about children but because they are among the 305 ballads included by Francis James Child (1825–1896) in his multivolume work, *The English and Scottish Popular Ballads* (1882–1898). Child wrote in 1882 that he had gathered "every valuable copy of every known ballad,"[10] a statement that can now be recognized as too optimistic. In his defense it can be said that, given his specific definitions, few other examples of ballads have been discovered in the nearly ninety years since his tenth, and last, volume appeared. This lack of success, however, may be in part because for much of this time no one was looking for new ballads of the Child type. Until very recently folksong collectors prized the Child ballads above all others and sought out mainly variants and versions of them and, in many instances, ignored everything else. This antiquarian attitude was pronounced as recently as 1956 when an Appalachian folklore collector proclaimed that "The genuine *ballad* is only one type of folksong. Your 'ballad' is not a true *folk* ballad unless it is closely kin to one of the 305— no more, no less!—in Professor Child's great collection."[11]

Broadsides are a second category of traditional balladry. These are songs originally printed on one side of a sheet of paper and sold for a small fee. Many of these ballads found in Anglo–American tradition are classified in G. Malcolm Laws's *American Balladry from British Broadsides* (1957). Generally speaking, the broadsides are of more recent vintage than the Child ballads. The latter date from roughly 1500–1750 while broadsides mostly date from 1650–1900, although there are exceptions on both sides of the line. The lyrics of Child ballads and broadsides are frequently compared to tabloids for, like them, both kinds of ballads often deal with sensational subjects—robberies, murders, and the like being among their most common themes. But, examples are better than discussions so, for purposes of illustration, two ballad texts are given below, the first a Child ballad and the second a broadside. In the first of these, "Earl Brand" (Child 7), a girl is carried off by her lover. Her father and seven brothers pursue them. The ballad text explains the rest of the story:

"Rise ye up, rise up my seven sons bold,
Put on your armour bright,
That it may not be said that a daughter of mine,
Can stay with Lord Thomas overnight."

"Lady Margaret, my love, be brave," cried he,
"Hold this rein in your white hand,
That I may fight your seven brothers bold,
As in yonders green meadow they stand."

Lady Margaret did watch the battle so grim,
She never shed one tear,
Until she saw her seven brothers fall,
And the father she loved so dear.

"Lady Margaret, my love, will you go, will you go?
Or will you here abide?"
"Oh I must go, Lord Thomas, you know,
You have left me now without a guide."

He placed Lady Margaret on the milk white steed,
Himself upon the bay,
Drew his buckler down by his side,
And then rode bleeding away.

Lord Thomas died of his bloody, bloody wounds,
Lady Margaret died of grief,
Lady Thomas died from the loss of her son,
The eleventh one that must be.

They buried Lord Thomas on the church's right side,
Lady Margaret they laid upon the left,
They would not be parted before they died,
And they were united in death.

Out of one grave grew a climbing rose,
Out of the other grew a briar,
They grew till they met at the top of the church,
And they did grow no higher.[12]

The second ballad, "The Boston Burglar," was published in 1888, with Michael J. Fitzpatrick credited as author, but it is thought to be of British broadside origin. Certainly it predates 1888 and is similar to various ballads about Botany Bay (a British penal colony in Australia that was especially feared) that were probably its prototype. At some point in time the city of Boston was substituted for London, perhaps as a means of Americanizing it. The present version has a further localization by bringing in the name of Little Rock, Arkansas, probably more meaningful to the singer, who lived 135 miles from the Arkansas town, than the city of Boston which is over 1000 miles away.

I was born in Boston City, boys,
A city you all know well.
Raised up by honest parents,
The truth to you I'll tell.
Raised up by honest parents,
Raised up most tenderly.
Till I became a sporting young man
At the age of twenty-three.

My character was token
And I was sent to jail.
Oh, the boys they found it all in vain
To get me out on bail.
The jury found me guilty,
The clerk he wrote it down.
Oh, the judge he passed a sentence, said he,
"You are bound for that Little Rock town."

They put me aboard this east-bound train
One cold December day.
And every station I'd pass through
I could hear those people say,
"There goes that Boston Burglar,
With iron strong chains he's bound down,
For some bad crime or other,
To be sent to that Little Rock town."

There lives a girl in Louisville,
A girl that I love well.
If ever I gain my liberty,
Along with her I'll dwell.
If ever I gain my liberty,
Bad company I will shun.
Likewise nightwalk and gambling,
And also drinking rum.

You who have your liberty;
Please keep it while you can.
And don't run around with boys at night
And break the laws of man.
For if you do you surely will
Find yourself like me,
Just serving out twenty-three long years
In the state penitentiary.[13]

Of course, not all Child ballads or broadsides deal with such serious matters. One of the more popular Child ballads in the South is "Our Goodman" (Child 274). This, and several other of the 305 Child pieces are comic numbers. The same can be said for the broadsides, an example of which is the following number of British origin that is known by various titles but called by the informant "Rich Old Lady."

I knew a rich old lady,
In London she did dwell.
She loved her husband dearly,
But other men twice as well.
Sing penny a wink she randolph,
Sing penny a wink she roan.

She went to the doctor
In hopes that she might find
Some kind of medicine
To make her husband blind.
Sing penny a wink she randolph,
Sing penny a wink she roan.

She gave him two marrow bones
And told him to suck them all.
And then he said, "My dear little wife
I cannot see you at all."
Sing penny a wink she randolph,
Sing penny a wink she roan.

"I think I'm going to drown myself,
If I only knew the way."
"Here, let me take you by the hand,
As you might go astray."
Sing penny a wink she randolph,
Sing penny a wink she roan.

Well, she walked on the banks,
And she walked on the shore.
And he said, "My dear little wife
You'll have to push me o'er."
Sing penny a wink she randolph,
Sing penny a wink she roan.

She took a few steps backwards
And run to push him in.
He just stepped to one side
And let her tumble in.
Sing penny a wink she randolph,
Sing penny a wink she roan.

Now, she began to holler,
And she began to squall.
But he said, "My dear little wife
I cannot see you at all."
Sing penny a wink she randolph,
Sing penny a wink she roan.

The old man being good-natured,
And afeared that she might swim,
He run and cut a big long pole
And pushed her further in.
Sing penny a wink she randolph,
Sing penny a wink she roan.

Now my little song is over
And I won't sing it no more.
But wasn't she a blamed old fool
For not swimming to the shore.[14]

One feature of many Child ballads found in the Old World that differs from the same songs found in the South, or elsewhere in the United States, is the elimination of magic and supernatural elements. For example, many Old World versions of "The Two Sisters" contain the supernatural motif of the singing instrument which is missing in most Southern versions. The first version of this ballad given in the body of the second volume of this collection is thus typical of Southern treatments. However, the "Wind and Rain" version also given here indicates that the supernatural elements of the ballad are not missing altogether in Southern renditions, although, even here, the singing instrument motif is greatly changed. There is nothing particularly magical about the instrument except that only one tune can be played on it. In older versions of "James Harris" (The Daemon Lover) (Child 243), which is commonly known in the South as "The House Carpenter" or "The House Carpenter's Wife," a revenant or the Devil comes to carry off a woman. As usually found in the South, the ballad simply describes a love triangle.

Along with the general tendency to eliminate supernatural and magic elements is a tendency to dispense with, or at least to diminish the importance of, sex, incest, and kin-murder. For example, older versions of "The Two Brothers" (Child 49) tell of jealousy arising because of an incestuous relationship with their sister. Southern versions, such as "Two Little Boys Were Going to School," typically have the brothers fight over a more trivial matter—the failure to play ball:

Two little boys were going to school,
And fine little boys were they.
I truly wish myself with them,
My playmates for to be.
I truly wish myself with them,
My playmates for to be.

Oh, Johnny can you toss the ball?
Or can you fling a stone?
I am too little, I am too young.
Dear brother leave me alone.
I am too little, I am too young.
Dear brother leave me alone.

Then Willie pulled out his pocket knife,
He had it keen and sharp.
Between the long ribs and the short
He pierced poor John to the heart,
Between the long ribs and the short
He pierced poor John to the heart.[15]

Obviously there are exceptions to these generalizations for there are Child ballads still traditional in the South that include supernatural elements, as the section of my second volume devoted to such songs clearly indicates. Usually the supernatural motifs are assumed without actually being stated.

Native American ballads, the third category of traditional ballads, are more numerous than either Child ballads or British broadsides and mostly date from 1850 to the present. There are exceptions, though, for "The Rattlesnake Song," which is given in Volume II, is thought to be considerably older. Like broadsides, the native American ballads deal largely with scandals and tragedies, although themes of American history and developments are also found. Then, too, there are many like "The Big Crap Game" which are merely humorous:

Well, I went out to a big crap game,
It was against my will.
Bet all my money
Except one greenback dollar bill.
Was a hundred dollars on the table,
And the feelings they were high.
Just then a cop came through the door
And I got mine.

I got mine, boys,
I got mine.
I grabbed that hundred dollars,
Through the window I did climb.
For a while I was a-wearin' good clothes,
Livin' on chicken and wine.
Was a leader in society
When I got mine.

Well, I went into a big cafe,
I went in there to dine,
I only had fifteen cents,
But was full of good white wine.
I ate everything on the table,
I was feelin' mighty fine.
And I handed over that fifteen cents
And I got mine.

I got mine, boys,
I got mine.
They used me for a football;
At kicking they was fine.
They kicked me through the window,
I got there just in time.
A policeman took me to the judge
And I got mine.

Well, I went to get some chickens,
The night was very fine.
I found them roostin' very high
And for them I did climb.
A bulldog came prowlin' round,
He got there just in time.
He got me by the seat of the pants
And he got mine.

He got mine, boys,
He got mine.
The rascal took my britches,
He did it very fine.
I went home in a barrel,
I got there just in time.
I used some Dr. Brown's Salve
Where he got mine.[16]

Several native American ballads, such as "The Fatal Wedding," are not cited in G. Malcolm Laws's *Native American Balladry* (1950; revised 1964), the standard bibliographic guide to these songs, because they are known to originate in the popular music industry. For the same reason such songs have often been overlooked by ballad collectors whose interest generally runs to older ballads of unknown authorship. In so doing they have slighted an important aspect of American balladry and, in a sense, distorted the picture of traditional singing in the United States.

Traditional ballads—whether Child, broadsides, or native American—all have distinctive characteristics. All three types generally concentrate on a single episode. Typical is the following version of "The Dying Brakeman" which focuses on a tragedy in which the motorman of a mine train is unable to stop the cars in time to prevent them from running over his brakeman:

> *See that true and trembling brakeman,*
> *As he falls between the cars!*
> *Not a moment's warning has he;*
> *From those freight cars he is hurled.*
>
> *See those car wheels passing o'er him,*
> *O'er his mangled body and head;*
> *See his sister bending o'er him,*
> *Crying, "Brother, are you dead?"*
>
> *"Dying, sister, yes, I'm dying;*
> *Going to join that other shore;*
> *For our father and our mother*
> *I shall never see no more.*
>
> *"Sister, when you see our brother,*
> *These few words I send to him;*
> *Never, never venture braking;*
> *If he does, his life will end."*[17]

Narratives in ballads are advanced primarily by means of dialogue. Some ballads are told entirely in dialogue but most alternate stanzas of dialogue with stanzas of action, with a bit of description mingled in. Typical is the following localized version of "The Gypsy Laddie" (Child 200), which is called, "When Carnal First Came to Arkansas":

> *When Carnal first came to Arkansas,*
> *He came from Missouri O.*
> *He sung so sweet and melodious*
> *That he charmed the heart of a lady O.*
>
> *When the landlord came in at night,*
> *Inquiring for his lady O,*
> *The answer was, "She is not here;*
> *She's run away with Carnal."*
>
> *Go saddle to me my little bay mare;*
> *The black is not so speedy O.*
> *I'll ride all day, I'll ride all night,*
> *Or I'll overtake my lady.*
>
> *Won't you turn around? Won't you come back?*
> *Won't you go with your husband O?*
> *I'll lock you up in a room so high,*
> *Where Carnal can't come nigh you.*
>
> *I won't turn around, nor I won't go back;*
> *I won't go with my husband O.*
> *I wouldn't give a kiss from Carnal's lips*
> *For all your land and your money.*

They rode east and they rode west;
They spent most all her money O.
Likewise the gold pins off her breast.
The gold rings off of her finger.

I used to have a house and home
And seven little babes to enthrall me O.
Now I've come to the want of bread,
And Carnal's gone and left me. [18]

The narrative approach in Child ballads is impersonal with little or no intrusion of the narrator's point of view. Even where the singer may be sympathetic with the protagonist's plight, such view is not explicitly stated. The same, to a lesser extent, can be said for both broadsides and native American ballads. Like modern journalism, ballads focus on the climax of an action and its result, giving the happenings in as straightforward, objective a manner as possible. The description of the duel in the version of "Little Massie Grove" (Child 81) contained in this book is a perfect example of the impersonality of the Child ballads as is this description of a murder in "Love Henry" (Child 68):

He went to the bed to little Marg'ret
And give her a farewell kiss.
And with a penknife in her right hand
She wounded him full death.
And with a penknife in her right hand
She wounded him full death. [19]

All of the preceding characteristics are typically found in Child ballads and are often present in broadsides and native American ballads as well. They can be considered primary characteristics while some other features found in many Child, and other types of, ballads are not essential. Many songs begin *in medias res,* that is, in the middle of the story. "The House Carpenter's Wife" (Child 243) which, in many versions, begins not with a detailed description of the scene but, rather, with the two principal figures greeting each other by saying "well met, well met" is a perfect example of this feature. The background is pieced together by the listener as the ballad progresses. Such a characteristic may reflect a loss during the process of transmission and reflects the tendency of ballads to retain only details that are absolutely essential.

Another characteristic often found in ballads is called leaping and lingering. This refers to the tendency to treat individual scenes in detail and then shift the narrative to another scene with little or no transition. Various kinds of repetition are also common; at least five different types occur regularly. These include plain repetition where words, phrases, or stanzas are simply repeated. There is also the climax of relatives in which songs consist largely and sometimes entirely of references to various members of one's family. "Jimmy Loud" and "Hangman" (Child 95) in this book are excellent examples of the climax of relatives. A third type of ballad repetition is incremental repetition in which the story is advanced by repeating nearly the same lines with minor changes that advance, or increment, the narrative. A perfect example of this type of repetition is the following version of "The Three Maids" (Child 11):

There was three maids a-playing ball, I lily-O
There was three maids a-playing ball, I lily-O
They some three lords for to court them all,
For the rose is sweet I know.

The foremost one was dressed in red, I lily-O
The foremost one was dressed in red,
And this is the one I make my wed,
For the rose is sweet I know.

The middle one was dressed in green, I lily-O
The middle one was dressed in green,
And this is the one I'll make my queen,
For the rose is sweet I know.

The foremost one was dressed in white, I lily-O
The foremost one was dressed in white,
Oh this is the one I'll make my wife,
For the rose is sweet I know.

Her brother John was standing by, I lily-O
Her brother John was standing by,
He wounded his sister with a knife
For the rose is sweet I know.

Ride on, ride on, to yonder's hill, I lily-O
Ride on, ride on, to yonder's hill,
Till I get down and bleed a while,
For the rose is sweet I know.

Ride on, ride on, to yonder's hill, I lily-O
Ride on, ride on, to yonder's hill,
Till I get down and make my will,
For the rose is sweet I know.

What do you will your sister Ann? I lily-O
What do you will your sister Ann?
My trunk of gold and silver pan,
For the rose is sweet I know.

What do you will your true love dear? I lily-O
What do you will your true love dear?
This snow white horse that I rode here,
For the rose is sweet I know.

What do you will your mother dear? I lily-O
What do you will your mother dear?
My snow white dress what I wore here,
For the rose is sweet I know.

Tell her to wash it nice and clean, I lily-O
Tell her to wash it nice and clean,
So my heart's blood can never be seen,
For the rose is sweet I know.[20]

Other types of ballad repetition include speech and action in which in one stanza a person is instructed to perform some action which he does in the next stanza. Finally, in some ballads a stanza is repeated, the repetition serving as a means of transition.

Many of these non-essential characteristics frequently occurring in Child ballads are often found in both broadsides and native American ballads. Broadsides, however, differ from Child ballads in that they frequently use the "Come all ye" opening stanza and are often narrated in the first person. Native American ballads are much more likely than the others to include a moral at the ending although older ballads have on several occasions been altered in Southern tradition to include comments of a moralizing nature. All three types of ballads generally have a short narrative, simple action, chronologically arranged scenes, a limited number of characters (usually two, rarely more than four), and hardly ever any action after the climax.

Having made these working definitions and outlined certain characteristics of ballads, it remains to note that ballads are not superorganic. That is, they do not exist by themselves but are, rather, kept alive by various singers. That may seem to be belaboring the obvious, yet at one time ballad collectors presented their texts as though they were maintained in some mysterious manner in which human beings played no part. Fortunately, that era is past, but even now most ballad collections have little more on the informant (the person the material was recorded from) than the name and date of collection. One of the shortcomings of the present volume is that in several cases I was unable to obtain anything more than the sketchiest data on informants. Whatever was available is given in the headnotes that precede each entry.

Granted that individual singers keep the ballads alive, the question arises: who are these ballad singers? What type of person maintains these traditions? The answer is, of course, that many different types of people are folk ballad singers. There is a certain degree of truth in the dogmatic claim set forth in 1951 by a prominent student of the ballad that folksingers are characterized by (1) living in a rural or isolated region which (2) "shuts [them] off from prolonged schooling and contact with industrialized urban civilization, so that (3) [their] cultural training is oral rather than visual."[21] He is correct because some traditional singers do meet all three of these requirements, but he is also wrong because many others do not. Indeed, if anything, the exceptions outweigh the rule. True, a singer like the late Almeda Riddle was from a rural background and did not have an extensive formal education. That does not mean that her whole cultural training was oral or that she had no knowledge of, or contact with, urban civilization. Anyone who ever met her knows that those characteristics simply didn't apply in her case.

For several of the informants Edwin Kirkland recorded in Tennessee during the 1930s and 1940s none of the three characteristics mentioned apply. His best sources of folk ballads were, in several instances, city residents who were highly educated, about whom it could not be said that their cultural training was entirely oral. For example, one of his best finds, a rare version of "Sir Patrick Spens" (Child 58), was collected in 1937 from Clara J. McCauley who had learned it from other members of her family. McCauley, the Supervisor of Public School Music in Knoxville, Tennessee, was an urban woman with an above average amount of formal education, hardly someone who could be described as a rustic illiterate out of contact with the modern world. Yet, her ballad was fully traditional by the strictest definition of folklore. Kirkland turned up many other good urban folk ballad singers, people like Columbus Popejoy, a Knoxville bank teller who was also a superb raconteur. Kirkland even found great traditional ballad singers among faculty members of the University of Tennessee. He recognized that, at the time, such settings were not where most people sought "songs in the genuine folk tradition," adding that "I held this opinion when I first began to collect, but before very long I found that faculty members not only were interested in folksongs but also had learned some of them in the true folk manner."[22] In all, roughly one third of Kirkland's large collection of folk ballads came from such highly educated, urban, but traditional singers as the University of Tennessee faculty or Clara McCauley.

Despite the evidence to the contrary the popular conception of a traditional balladeer is that of a rustic, unschooled illiterate. As already mentioned it was once the view of most ballad scholars and, even today, has a few adherents in the academic world, admittedly mainly among those who don't do fieldwork. Yet, if the bulk of evidence refutes such a view why has it persisted? There are, of course, many possible explanations. One is that academics like to view things in black and white terms when, in actuality, most things are gray. There is, in other words, a tendency to offer the perfect example as the only example. There is no doubt about the folk nature of someone who lives removed from contact with everything but the "purest" folk cultures. It seems doubtful that any such society, or even person, ever existed in America. A second possible reason for the longevity of the rustic, unschooled illiterate concept of ballad singers is simply that it is romantic and somehow exotic to think of the folk as being creatures who are colorful and live in picturesque bucolic settings. The folk ballad singer has, in some cases, replaced the noble savage of past centuries. There is also the unfortunate fact that some collectors and authorities tend to view the folk as inferiors who are to be pitied and, in most cultural situations, avoided. It is worth noting here that ballad singers are also often stereotyped as being poor. To those holding this view the folk are always seen as someone different from themselves, charmingly quaint but also somehow disgusting people who must be consigned to some place other than that in which most people live. Finally, the rustic illiterate concept of folk ballad singers is often perpetuated because the tacit assumption is made that "folk," "popular," and "academic" culture are three distinct levels which never interact. Thus, one can function on only one level at a time and they exist in tiers with "folk" culture at the bottom and "academic" culture at the top. In reality all three levels are on the same tier and there is interaction between them all the time, thus it is possible to function in more than one area simultaneously. Contrary to the stereotype, folksingers are found everywhere, from the most rural to the most urban settings. They do not exist in a world that no one else inhabits but function, for better or worse, in the same world all of us live in. Briefly put, geographic area, financial status, educational background, political inclinations, or other similar factors have nothing to do with determining whether or not a person is a ballad singer. No matter where or how they live, ballad singers are intelligent people with good memories who have an interest in, and are willing to sing ballads.

There are many people blessed with intelligence and good memories who have an interest in ballads but simply aren't good ballad singers. They are what the Swedish folklorist Carl Wilhelm von Sydow labeled *passive bearers of tradition.* Unlike active tradition bearers "the passive bearers have indeed heard of what a certain tradition contains, and may perhaps when questioned, recollect part of it, but do nothing themselves to spread it or keep it alive."[23] It seems that Dorothy Oswald, a student at the University of Arkansas, from whom Irene Carlisle collected a version of "The Great Titanic," was such a passive traditional ballad singer. She gave Carlisle the words to the song, which she had from traditional sources, and even recalled the melody but did not sing it even though she was aware of the collector's interest in obtaining melodies for the songs she gathered. On the other hand, the late Fred High, one of Arkansas's best known traditional singers, was in every sense a person who helped "keep tradition alive and transmit it,"[24] even going so far as printing seventy-three of the ballads he knew in a small paperback book which was sold primarily in the area around his home near Berryville, Arkansas. High had a keen sense of the value of the ballads he knew and sang for his own community and was always willing to sing for collectors. As a result numerous recordings of his singing are available today in various folklore archives.

Passive bearers of ballads, as well as other types of folklore, do play a significant role. Von Sydow noted that passive carriers of a tradition give it resonance. That is, they reinforce and prolong a tradition by providing it with an audience. It is, of course, possible for a singer to sit and sing ballads to himself but it is not likely that the songs are going to remain in tradition long if the singer is his sole audience. Passive bearers also act, to some extent, as a check on tradition. If, for example, some change is made in a ballad the passive singer, being familiar with the song, can easily correct it, "and they do so, which is of great importance for the unchanging survival of the tradition."[25]

A not uncommon situation is for passive and active bearers to change their relationship to folk tradition. Passive bearers might become active if they hear a tradition long enough that they become conversant with it and take it actively in hand. On the other hand, active bearers may become passive for various reasons. For example, a child may know several children's folksongs but become passive concerning them once he has outgrown his childhood. As noted above, an active bearer may also become passive when there is no longer an audience for the traditions he knows. Usually, though, active and passive ballad singers remain so all their lives.

Granted that there are both active and passive ballad singers, where do they perform? What is the environment in which folk ballads are sung? The answer is simple: they are sung just about anywhere, although generally before an audience of at least one other person besides the singer. Unlike some other genres of folklore, such as the proverb or legend, ballads often are performed by a singer for his own enjoyment in situations where no one else is around. In most instances, though, there is some other audience involved, typically a small one. Usually the distance between the singer and the audience is not so great as that between a concert pianist and those attending his recital. There is also often much more interplay between the singer and audience than is commonly the case in formal concerts.

Almeda Riddle (1898–1986) related an amusing incident concerning the effect her singing had on one audience. It is quoted here in full not only because it shows the context of some ballad singing but also because it reveals much about the typical relationship between a folksinger and the audience. "I remember one time we were picking cotton— as a child I was in the cotton patch—I think I was seven years old at the time and I'd first heard this 'No Telephone in Heaven,' and I sang it over and over all day long. I couldn't think of anything else until finally a man offered me a quarter. Now, a quarter at that time—as a child twenty-five cents meant as much as a dollar and a half would mean to a child now. Well, this man, he gave me twenty-five cents if I would please just not sing 'No Telephone in Heaven' again that day. And the next day I could sing it all I wanted to."[26]

Given that traditional ballad singers perform just about anywhere, the question remains: why do they sing ballads? Again, it is relatively easy to answer the query even though until approximately twenty-five years ago most collectors did not bother to ask their informants about such matters. Still, the clues that do exist suggest a myriad of reasons, almost as many as one can imagine. Among the most important are that a singer likes the story told in a ballad's lyrics, or likes the tune, or both. Some see it as a way of preserving their own past; others think of ballads as an important, and fun, portion of local history. For example, a ballad like "Lula Viers" in Volume II may be to the traditional singer from Kentucky an accurate account of a local tragedy. Often a ballad is kept alive because it was associated with a beloved person close to the singer. Sometimes the ballad is perpetuated because of the lesson it teaches, sometimes because it is considered a classic. There are, of course, many other possibilities but these are sufficient to make the point that there is no single reason that explains why traditional singers perform ballads.

Almeda Riddle provided a good capsule summary of why she chose the songs she sings. Speaking of "classic" ballads she said: "A classic ballad is something you class highly, something in your idea. Maybe what someone else would call a classic I wouldn't. 'Lady Margaret,' a nice version of it, I think that's a classic. This 'Four Marys' I consider that one too—to me, maybe not to you. And a variant of this 'Hangman's Tree' that is very old—I found this back in about, I believe, in about the fifteenth century in an old Scottish book. And almost this version. Almost exactly like this is, and I'd been singing it then for forty years.

"But I don't think the age has everything to do with a classic. You might write a classic. Something that would be classical—would teach something, be worth preserving. It could be dirty and old and trash and not teach anything and be a thousand years old and still would be that when it started out. That's what the word 'classic' to me means. That teaches something that's worth remembering, that's worth passing on."[27]

One other consideration concerning ballad singers merits attention, namely the manner in which they perform. Any folksinger or, for that matter, anyone who is an active bearer of any kind of folklore, presents his material in a specific manner. Southern traditional singers perform in an impersonal or objective style. The singers maintain one tempo, one level of intensity, one timbre throughout a song. They remain, in a sense, detached from the lyrics and never resort to any intrusions that detract from the ballad. A routine stanza providing plot background is given equal attention with a stanza that contains the dramatic climax. No sudden diminuendo (lowering of volume) or crescendo (increasing volume), such as the art or popular singer employs to spotlight important points in a song, is used. For traditional ballad singers in the South, as elsewhere in America, the text is of major importance; all else is secondary. When, in "Barbara Allen," William calls her to his deathbed, the meeting would be treated by the art singer as a very significant part of the song, its importance emphasized by the use of such musical dynamics as diminuendos or crescendos or ritardandos (slowing down), whereas the folk singer treats these stanzas no differently than any other in the ballad.

All that remains is some explanation of the categories used in the present book. Basically they follow the categories outlined in the two books by G. Malcolm Laws, *American Balladry From British Broadsides* and *Native American Balladry,* the standard bibliographic guides to all American folk balladry but, as any observer can tell, do not follow them exclusively. The changes were necessitated by the material that I was able to accumulate from other sources in a relatively short time. I am fully aware that arranging the ballads by textual considerations tends to ignore the importance of ballad music, but in my defense I offer the argument that it is the method most often used by editors of ballad collections and therefore has tradition on its side. Moreover, I am fully aware that ballads are not superorganic, that they are kept alive in tradition by people. These categories are offered only as a convenient means of ordering the material at hand, not as an ironclad arrangement of texts. Indeed, some songs could just as easily be placed in another category than the one it is given in here, but that is also a problem with the Laws categories. Despite the admitted flaws of this method of presentation, I believe it does include the major themes of Southern folk balladry. One other note of caution: a low number of selections given here under a specific category does not necessarily indicate the degree of popularity of that theme in Southern folk balladry, but only shows that I was unable to obtain a larger supply of songs on that particular topic in time for inclusion.

All of the ballads in this first volume are given under seven headings: war ballads, ballads of crime and criminals, ballads of family opposition to lovers, ballads of lovers' disguises and tricks, ballads of faithful lovers, ballads of unfaithful lovers, and ballads of cowboys and pioneers. Some readers may find the section of ballads of cowboys and pioneers controversial because it includes some items assigned elsewhere by Laws. They should keep in mind my remarks about the reasons for my categories, and also that neither these nor Laws's groupings are without flaws.

The main reason for putting together a collection of ballads is to have people read, enjoy, and, if they wish, sing them. To facilitate singing I have included, wherever possible, a melody transcription, in a few cases taking a melody line from some other source than the person whose text is given here. In all those instances where no melody line is given there was none available to me either from collector, informant, or alternative source. Those texts with melodies provided from alternative sources are clearly indicated; in all other cases the melody is as sung by the informant who is identified. The accompanying headnotes provide historical information on each ballad.

One final comment: it is customary for editors of folksong and ballad collections to lament the passing of these items. Such volumes are often presented in a funerary spirit that would lead one to believe that the gems they contain were destined to disappear from earth forever. That is not the attitude of the present editor, who hopes this collection will demonstrate that folk balladry is not only alive in the South but is flourishing. True, it probably doesn't exist in the same way it did in eighteenth-century England, but then, folk balladry of that era was not exactly the same as that found in England two centuries earlier. Folk ballad singing has undergone change in the past and most likely will again, but it is a long way from being dead. In fact, the almost constant change, enabling Southern folk balladry to adapt to changing conditions, may be the one thing that has insured the survival of the tradition.

W.K. McNeil
THE OZARK FOLK CENTER

[1]For a more detailed discussion of these points, see my book *The Charm Is Broken: Readings in Arkansas and Missouri Folklore* (Little Rock: August House, Inc., 1984), pp. 11–13.

[2]On the matter of where "the South" is see John Shelton Reed, *The Enduring South: Subcultural Persistence in Mass Society* (Chapel Hill: The University of North Carolina Press, 1982) and the same author's *Southerners: The Social Psychology of Sectionalism* (Chapel Hill: The University of North Carolina Press, 1983). The states I have included in "the South" do not entirely agree with a table given in *The Enduring South,* p. 16, but Reed notes, p. 14, that persons involved in the survey were not asked to comment on whether Kentucky was a Southern state or not.

[3]Collected in 1979 by W.K. McNeil from Bob Blair, Pleasant Grove, Arkansas. Blair's version of the song can be heard on *Not Far From Here . . . : Traditional Tales and Songs Recorded in the Arkansas Ozarks.* Arkansas Traditions, no number.

[4]Collected in 1979 by W.K. McNeil from Rance Blankenship, Melbourne, Arkansas. Blankenship's version can be heard on *Not Far From Here.*

[5]Collected May 14, 1963 by Mrs. Robert J. Snyder from the singing of Mrs. Deans Crumpler and Susan Harriet Snyder, Columbia, South Carolina.

[6]*Ibid.*

[7]Text quoted from Roger D. Abrahams and George Foss, *Anglo–American Folksong Style* (Englewood Cliffs, New Jersey: Prentice–Hall, Inc., 1968), pp. 40–41.

[8]Shenstone is quoted in volume III of *The Frank C. Brown Collection of North Carolina Folklore* (Durham: Duke University Press, 1952), p. 3.

[9]See Brown, III, 275 and Celeste P. Cambiaire, *East Tennessee and Western Virginia Mountain Ballads* (London: The Mitre Press, 1935), p. 37.

[10]Francis J. Child, *The English and Scottish Popular Ballads,* I (New York: Dover Publications, Inc., 1965; reprint of a work originally issued in 1882), vii.

[11]Richard Chase, *American Folk Tales and Songs* (New York: The New American Library of World Literature, Inc., (1956), p. 229.

[12]Collected by George Foss in 1961 from Robert Shiflett, Brown's Cove, Virginia.

[13]Collected by W.K. McNeil, August, 1977 from Rance Blankenship, Melbourne, Arkansas. Blankenship can be heard singing the song on *Not Far From Here.*

[14]Collected in 1979 by W.K. McNeil from Kenneth Rorie, Batesville, Arkansas. Rorie can be heard singing the song on *Not Far From Here.*

[15]Collected by W.K. McNeil, April 25, 1979, from Mrs. Alice Best, Fox, Arkansas.

[16]Collected by W.K. McNeil in 1979 from Bob Blair, Pleasant Grove, Arkansas. Blair can be heard singing the song on *Not Far From Here.*

[17]Collected by Irene Jones Carlisle, June 29, 1951, from Lewis Bedingfield, Springdale, Arkansas.

[18]Collected by Theodore R. Garrison, July, 1942, from Mrs. Zona Baker, Zack, Arkansas.

[19]Collected by George Foss in 1958 from Marybird McAllister, Brown's Cove, Virginia.

[20]Collected by Herbert Halpert, Emory L. Hamilton, and an unidentified woman, March 24, 1939, from Polly Johnson, Wise, Virginia. Johnson can be heard singing the song on *Virginia Traditions: Ballads From British Tradition* BRI-002.

[21]Joseph W. Hendron, "The Scholar and the Ballad Singer," in MacEdward Leach and Tristram P. Coffin, *The Critics and the Ballad* (Carbondale and Edwardsville: Southern Illinois University Press, 1961), p. 7. Hendron's article originally appeared in *The CEA Critic.*

[22]Quoted in the booklet accompanying Tennessee Folklore Society album TFS-106 *The Kirkland Recordings*, p. 3.

[23]C.W. von Sydow, *Selected Papers of Folklore* (New York: Arno Press, 1977; reprint of a work originally published in 1948), pp. 12–13.

[24]See Carlisle's M.A. thesis *Fifty Ballads and Songs From Northwest Arkansas* submitted at the University of Arkansas in 1952, p. 84.

[25]von Sydow, p. 14.

[26]Roger D. Abrahams, *A Singer and Her Songs: Almeda Riddle's Book of Ballads* (Baton Rouge: Louisiana State University Press, 1970), pp. 108–109.

[27]*Ibid.*, pp. 109, 111.

War Ballads

The Green Willow Tree

COLLECTED BY IRENE J. CARLISLE, MARCH 9, 1951, FROM RACHEL HENRY, SPRING
VALLEY, ARKANSAS.   TRANSCRIPTION BY DOROTHY OSWALD.

There was a little ship that sailed on the sea,
Crying, "Oh, the lonesome, the lowland low!"
There was a little ship that sailed on the sea;
It went by the name of the *Green Willow Tree*,
That was sailing on the lonesome lowland low,
That was sailing on the lonesome sea.

It hadn't been sailing there in a half a year or more,
Crying, "Oh, the lonesome, the lowland low!"
It hadn't been sailing there in a half a year or more,
Till it was overtook by a Turkey *Shevelee*
That was sailing on the lowland lonesome low,
That was sailing on the lonesome sea.

"Captain, oh, Captain, what will we do?"
Crying, "Oh, the lonesome, the lowland low!"
"Captain, oh, Captain, what will we do?
It'll run right over us and cut us in two,
And'll sink us in the lonesome, the lowland low,
And'll sink us in the lonesome sea."

"Captain oh, Captain, what'll you give me?"
Crying, "Oh, the lonesome, the lowland low!"
"Captain, oh, Captain, what'll you give me
To overtake and sink that Turkey *Shevelee*
That's a-sailing on the lonesome lowland low,
That's a-sailing on the lonesome sea?"

"I'll give you money and I'll set you free,"
Crying, "Oh, the lonesome, the lowland low!"
"I'll give you money and I'll set you free;
Besides, my eldest daughter your be-wedded wife shall be,
If you'll sink 'em in the lonesome lowland low,
If you'll sink 'em in the lonesome sea."

He down upon his breast, and away swam he,
Crying, "Oh, the lonesome, the lowland low!"
He down upon his breast, and away swam he,
And he soon overtook that Turkey *Shevelee*
That's a-sailing on the lonesome lowland low,
That's a-sailing on the lonesome sea.

Having a tool that was fit for to use,
Crying, "Oh, the lonesome, the lowland low!"
Having a tool that was fit for to use,
He bored seven holes which let in the juice
That'd sink 'em in the lonesome lowland low,
That'd sink 'em in the lonesome sea.

Some with their hats and some with their caps,
Crying, "Oh, the lonesome, the lowland low!"
Some with their hats and some with their caps,
Trying for to stop those large water-gaps
That would sink 'em in the lonesome lowland low,
That'd sink 'em in the lonesome sea.

He down upon his breast and away swam he,
And he soon overtook the *Green Willow Tree*,
That was sailing on the lonesome lowland low,
That was sailing on the lonesome sea.

"Captain, oh, Captain, you take me on board?"
Crying, "Oh, the lonesome, the lowland low!"
"Captain, oh, Captain, you take me on board,
Or will you be as good as your word?
For I'm sinking in the lonesome sea."

"No, sir, no sir, not take you on board,"
Crying, "Oh, the lonesome, the lowland low!"
"No, sir, no sir, not take you on board,
Nor neither will I be as good as my word;
For I'll sink you in the lonesome sea."

"If it wasn't for the sake of those on board,"
Crying, "Oh, the lonesome, the lowland low!"
"If it wasn't for the sake of those on board
I'd sink you in the lonesome sea."

He down upon his back and away sank he,
Crying, "Oh, the lonesome, the lowland low!"
Down upon his back and away sank he;
"Adieu, adieu to the *Green Willow Tree,*
That's a-sailing in the lonesome lowland low,
That's a-sailing on the lonesome sea."

Among the most widely traveled of the 305 songs Francis James
Child included in his monumental work, *The English and Scottish Popular
Ballads* (1882–1898), is the one he assigned number 286 and called "The
Sweet Trinity." It is known traditionally by many other titles including
"The Golden Vanity," "Cabin Boy," "The Cruise in the Lowlands Low,"
"The Lonesome Sea," "The Lowlands Low," "The Turkish Reveille,"
"Merry Golden Tree," and the one used for this version which was
collected by Irene J. Carlisle from Rachel Henry, Spring Valley, Arkansas,
March 9, 1951. The prototype of this ballad is an early seventeenth cen-
tury broadside included in volume four of Samuel Pepys' *Ballads* (1682–
1685), that recounts the exploits of a cabin boy on board one of Sir Walter
Raleigh's ships. In America, Sir Walter Raleigh is rarely connected with
the song while the ship has various names ranging from "Golden Vanity"
to "Merry Golden Tree" to "Turkish Traveloo" among others.

American versions also differ from the Sir Walter Raleigh broadside
in their conclusion. In a number of texts collected in the United States
the cabin boy gallantly refuses to follow his inclination to sink the ship
after the captain goes back on his word. This touch is wholly American,
as are the endings in which justice is achieved by various means. For
example, in some versions the protagonist dies after the captain refuses
to keep his word but the cabin boy's ghost returns to haunt the captain.
In other versions the crew throws the captain overboard and drowns him
after he refuses to keep his word to the hero. In a more elaborate text a
storm arises after the lad dies and he speaks from Heaven telling the
captain he will sink the ship. This threat is carried out and the captain
drowns.

There is now no certain way to find out exactly when "The Sweet
Trinity" first migrated to the New World but at least one authority,
Phillips Barry, believed it came across at the time of the big American
immigration. Certainly, its present popularity is attributable not only to
oral tradition but records as well, for several old-time groups, such as the
original Carter Family, recorded the song.

Rachel Henry was born at Brush Creek, a rural community near
Springdale, Arkansas, and spent her entire life in that neighborhood. Her
parents separated before her birth, and she adopted her mother's maiden
name of Briggs. Most of her songs were learned from young people in her

community, when she was a girl. Her version of "The Sweet Trinity" she learned in the 1890s from Jody Ragsdale, her sister's sweetheart. Mrs. Henry was said to be a jolly woman who took great delight in her singing. She would often forget parts of her songs but go right on chanting what she thought was the story until she recalled it all. She was in her seventies when the text given here was recorded by Irene J. Carlisle.

James Bird

COLLECTED JUNE 10, 1951 BY IRENE J. CARLISLE FROM ANNIE CAGLE, WOOLSEY, ARKANSAS. TRANSCRIPTION BY DOROTHY OSWALD.

Sons of freedom, listen to me,
And ye daughters, all give ear;
You a sad and mournful story
As was ever told shall hear.

Hull, you know his troops surrendered,
And defenseless left the West;
Then our forces quick assembled,
The invader to resist.

Among troops that marched to Erie
Were the Kingstown volunteers;
Captain Thomas then commander,
To protect our west frontiers.

Tender were the scenes of parting;
Mothers wrung their hands and cried,
Maidens wept their sways in secret,
Fathers strove their tears to hide.

There was one among our number,
Tall and gallant was his mien,
Firm his step, his look undaunted;
Scarce a nobler youth was seen.

One sweet kiss he snatched from Mary,
Craved his mother's prayer once more,
Pressed his father's hand, and left them
For Lake Erie's distant shore.

Mary tried to say, "Farewell, James."
Waved her hand, but nothing spake.
"Goodbye, Bird; may Heaven protect you
From the crowd at Parting Brake."

Soon he came to where noble Perry
Had assembled all his fleet;
There the gallant Bird enlisted,
Expecting soon the foe to meet.

Where is Bird? The battle rages;
Is he in the strife, or no?
Now the cannon roars tremendous;
Dare he meet the hostile foe?

See, behold him there with Perry;
In the selfsame ship they fight;
Though his mates all fall around him,
Nothing can his soul afright.

But behold, a ball has struck him;
See the crimson current flow;
"Leave the deck!" exclaimed brave Perry;
"No!" cried Bird. "I will not go!"

"Here on deck I took my station;
Ne'er will Bird his colors fly;
I'll stand by you, gallant captain,
Till we conquer or I die."

Still he fought, though faint and bleeding;
Still the stars and stripes arose;
Victory having crowned our efforts,
All triumphant o'er our foes.

Then did Bird receive a pension?
Was he to his friends restored?
No, nor ever to his bosom
Clasped the maid his heart adored.

"Dearest parents," said the letter,
"This will bring sad news to you;
Do not mourn your first beloved,
Though this brings his last adieu.

"I must suffer for deserting
Off the bridge at Nigaree;
Read this letter, brother, sister;
It's the last you'll have from me."

Sad and gloomy was the morning
Bird was ordered out to die;
Where's the breast not dead to pity
But for him would heave a sigh?

See him march and bear his fetters;
Harsh the clank upon the ear,
But his step is firm and manly,
For his heart ne'er harbored fear.

See him kneel upon his coffin,
Sure his death can do no good;
Spare him! Oh, God, they've shot him;
See his bosom stream with blood.

Farewell, Bird, farewell forever;
Home and friends you'll see no more,
But his mangled corpse lies buried
On Lake Erie's distant shore.

This ballad is usually thought of as being a Northern song but it has been collected occasionally in the South. Versions have been recorded from traditional singers in North Carolina, West Virginia, Texas, and this text sung by Annie Cagle, Woolsey, Arkansas, June 10, 1951. Actually, Cagle not only sang the ballad for collector Irene Carlisle, she also wrote it down afterwards and it is her verbatim text that is given here.

"James Bird" is an accurate account of the naval career of a hero of the War of 1812 who was later executed for desertion. His bravery under Commodore Oliver Hazard Perry (1785–1819) at the Battle of Lake Erie is praised in glowing terms but his later desertion from the brig *Niagara,* Perry's flagship, is glossed over. The last six verses deal with Bird's execution in 1814 and his subsequent burial. In its emphases and sympathy for Bird, Cagle's version is typical of most American examples of the ballad.

Unlike some songs dealing with the War of 1812 ("Hunters of Kentucky," for example) "James Bird" was written shortly after the events it describes. Its author, Charles Miner, was a Congressman, editor, and man of affairs, who published it in 1814 in his newspaper *The Gleaner* at Wilkes–Barre, Pennsylvania. The farewell letter Bird wrote to his family was dated November 9, 1814, so Miner's ballad appeared within a month after the hero's death. Although Miner wrote no further songs that made it into oral tradition, his one "hit" has lasted in the memories of folksingers for more than a century and a half.

Annie Cagle was fifty-six years old at the time she contributed

"James Bird" to Irene Carlisle. Born in Iconium, Missouri, in 1895, Cagle moved to Ozark, Arkansas when she was a small girl shortly after the turn of the century. The family moved to Fayetteville about 1927 and Cagle spent most of her adult life with her husband on a chicken farm near Woolsey, Arkansas. A woman with a good memory, Mrs. Cagle is said to have had a strong, sweet voice. She learned "James Bird" from a Mrs. Walter Smith of Iconium, Missouri, who claimed that her grandfather was a member of the firing squad that executed Bird. At the time of recording, Cagle had known the ballad for over forty years.

Tom Halyard

COLLECTED JUNE 4, 1950 BY GEORGE W. BOSWELL FROM MRS. STANLEY HORN, NASHVILLE, TENNESSEE.   TRANSCRIPTION BY GEORGE W. BOSWELL.

Now the rage of battle ended
And the foe for mercy called,
Death no more with smoke and thunder
Rolled upon the vengeful ball.

From the main deck to the quarter,
Strewn with limbs and wet with blood,
Poor Tom Halyard, pale and wounded,
Crawled to where his captain stood.

"Oh, my noble captain, tell me,
Ere I'm borne a corpse away,
Have I done a seaman's duty
On this great, this glorious day?

"Tell a dying sailor truly,
For my life is fleeting fast,
Have I done a seaman's duty?
Can there aught my memory blast?"

"Oh, brave Tom," replied the captain,
"Thou a sailor's part hast done.
I regret thy wounds with sorrow,
Wounds by which our glory's won."

"Thanks, my captain. Life is ebbing
Fast from this deep-wounded heart,
Yet, oh, grant one little favor
Ere I from this world depart.

"Bid some kind and trusty sailor,
When I'm numbered with the dead,
For my true, my constant Catherine,
Cut a lock from this poor head.

"Bid him to my Catherine bear it,
Saying, 'Here's a lonely die.'
Kate will keep the mournful present
And embalm it with a sigh."

"That I will," replied the captain,
"And be ever Catherine's friend."
"Thanks, my good, my great commander.
Now my pain, my sorrows end."

Mute, toward the captain weeping,
Tom upraised a thankful eye,
Grateful now his feet embracing,
Sank with "Kate!" on his last sigh.

Although textually this ballad seems like a British broadside ballad, its precise history is unknown. The melody line is unusual for a folk song in that it modulates from a beginning like G major or E minor to an ending like D major. It was collected June 4, 1950 by George W. Boswell from Mrs. Stanley Horn, Nashville, Tennessee. She learned it from her grandmother, Mrs. William (Lucinda) Rear, who was born while her family was traveling west from Virginia. Mrs. Rear also had a hand-written "ballet" of the piece.

COLLECTED MAY 30, 1962 BY GEORGE FOSS FROM ROBERT SHIFLETT, BROWNS COVE, VIRGINIA. TRANSCRIPTION BY DAN BRACKIN.

Come all ye Texas Rangers wherever you may be,
I'll tell to you a story that happened unto me.
One night the age of fifteen years I joined a royal band,
We marched from San Antonio unto the Rio Grande.

And yet the captain told us,
Perhaps he thought it right,
"Before we reach the station, boys,
I'm sure we'll have to fight."

We saw the Indians coming,
We heard them give their yell;
My feelings at that moment
No tongue could ever tell.

We saw their glittering lances,
Their arrows round us hailed.
My heart was sink [sic] within me,
My courage almost failed.

I thought of my old mother,
Who in tears to me did say:
"To you they all are strangers,
With me you'd better stay."

I thought her weak and childish,
And that she did not know,
For I was bent on roaming
And I was bound to go.

We fought them full five hours
Before the fight gave o'er.
Three hundred of our soldiers
Lay weltering in their gore.

Three hundred noble rangers
As ever trod the West,
We laid them by their comrades,
Sweet peace to be their rest.

Perhaps you have a mother,
Likewise a sister too,
And maybe so a sweetheart
To weep and mourn for you.

If this should be your condition,
And you are bound to roam,
I advise you from experience
You'd better stay at home.

Although this song is of native American origin it is thought to be derived in part from various British broadsides of the early nineteenth century. It bears closest resemblance to "Nancy of Yarmouth" but has some elements in common with "Sea Storm" and "President Parker." Still, it is not taken wholecloth from these sources and since most of the similarities are of the type that are found in many ballads, proving direct connections is difficult. That the precise history of the song has not been traced makes definite statements about derivation even more risky. Henry Belden thought the ballad was inspired by the battle at the Alamo in 1836 but that is just speculation. That no extant version speaks of the enemy as Mexicans decreases, but doesn't necessarily refute, the probability suggested by Belden. Certainly the ballad was in oral circulation by the second half of the nineteenth century, possibly as early as the 1860s. No known version can be dated prior to 1880 although several that can't be definitely dated are probably of earlier vintage. Some versions refer to the enemy as Yankees or Rebels rather than Indians, suggesting that it was known during the Civil War.

Generally the ballad is called "The Texas Rangers" (sometimes the singular is used) but "Texican Ranger," "Longstreet's Rangers," "Gallant Ranger," and "Come All Ye Southern Soldiers" are also used traditionally. Except for the name of the enemy there is little variation in the story. Most texts are eight stanzas long, so the present version is a bit lengthier than is usual for this ballad. The song is historically accurate, for the Texas Rangers were originally formed to protect settlers from Indians; later they occupied themselves with local outlaws and ultimately came to be regarded in many quarters in much the same way as the FBI.

The present text was collected May 30, 1962 by George Foss from Robert Shiflett, Browns Cove, Virginia. Shiflett (1905–1979) was born in "Shiflett Hollow" in Greene County, Virginia. His father, Erasmus, was a storekeeper in the area and the family moved to the mouth of Browns Cove in Albemarle County when Robert was a young child. Shiflett was known locally as "Raz's Robert" since he was the son of Erasmus. He was the brother-in-law of Mary Woods Shiflett, the widow of his oldest brother, who also contributed several ballads and songs to Foss. The source of Shiflett's version of "Texas Rangers" is not indicated.

Ballads of Crime and Criminals

The Ballad of the Braswell Boys

RECORDED BY JESSE HUDELSTON, COOKEVILLE, TENNESSEE, 1976. TRANSCRIPTION
BY W. K. McNEIL.

Come my friends and near relations,
Come and listen to my song,
I will sing about the Braswell's,
About the men who were hung.

On the twenty-ninth of November,
Eighteen and seventy-five,
Was the night they done the murder
For which they had to give their lives.

They said, dear father and dear mother,
I hope will remember me,
When we are dead and gone forever,
And our faces no more you'll see.

When I rise and fly to glory,
I will meet my Savior there;
I shall live and reign forever,
Shall we know each other there?

We have lain long in prison,
In our attempt we never fail,
God will aid and assist us
For to break the Nashville jail.

When they started from prison,
And the guards surrounded them,
Teek said, "Joe we are lost forever,
For our escape is very slim."

Dear parents and sister and brothers,
For my soul do understand,
I am bound for to acknowledge
That I am a guilty man.

I want you all to go to the meeting,
Lead new lives from this day,
For I expect to go to Heaven,
I can with you no longer stay.

Bohannon placed them in a wagon,
They were neat and very young,
Their coffins were seats for them
To the place where they were hung.

They had a sister and a brother
That seemed so very nigh,
They followed down to the hollow
Where they soon did see them die.

When they ascended the scaffold,
And the guards surrounded them,
They were joined by McFerrin,
Who opened up their prayer for them.

The third chapter of Romans,
It was read to them there;
And in a private conversation
They poured out their souls in prayer.

Death, you know, is the wages
You receive for your sins,
You must learn that in the future
You have to lose all you win.

Do not drink a drop of whiskey,
Do not kill or rob a man,
For it was the love of money
That I do on the gallows stand.

We know they committed murder
By taking other lives away,
So now upon this solemn hour
We must take theirs today.

Then Joe said, in a cool voice,
"Gentleman and ladies, too,
If you will give me your attention,
I will speak some words to you.

I am here upon the scaffold
Before you all today,
And what's it for? It is for murder,"
Was the words he did say.

"What caused me to do this murder?
It was whiskey and money, too,
And if you drink a drop of whiskey
Whiskey then might tempt you."

Teek said: "It's a solemn hour,
It's told me that I must die,
I am ready and awaiting,
Prepared and will to die."

Then Isbell came upon the scaffold
Shaking hands with them there;
They were delighted at his presence,
Seemed very glad to meet him there.

He said, "Joe, was you at my house
The night the murder was done?"
"I was there and I am guilty,"
Was the answer Joe made him.

Teek was low and fair complected,
Joe was tall and very neat,
They were pale and very silent
When their lips did seem to meet.

They listened to the death sentence,
It was there read to them,
Then they tied their wrists and ankles
And placed white caps upon them.

One said: "Jesus do have mercy
Will you be with me today?"
The other said, "Lord, have mercy
On them that swore my life away."

The door fell and left them swinging
Betwixt the earth and the sky
It was for a dreadful murder
That two men did have to die.

They were cut down, put in their coffins,
Delivered over to their friends,
That was there for the purpose
To receive them at the end.

Read this song while you are adorning
When you before the judgment stand,
You by this might take warning,
Live only a sober man.

Do not keep any bad company,
I advise you not to drink a dram
Or you might be like the brothers
That did on the gallows stand.

On November 29, 1875, George "Teek" and Joe Braswell, along with two other relatives, killed Russell and John Allison in Putnam County, Tennessee while in the act of committing a robbery. J.B. Allison, a relative of the murdered men, was sheriff of Putnam County and he arrested the Braswells. Rumors of a planned jailbreak led to a decision to transport Teek and Joe to Nashville for safekeeping. At the subsequent trial they were convicted and sentenced to death, an act that was carried out in Cookeville, March 27, 1878. Joe admitted his guilt but Teek maintained his innocence to the last and, according to newspaper reports of the time, tried to hold on to the jail when it was time for him to go to his execution.

There was nothing particularly unusual about the crime, but a ballad written about the case by an anonymous author is somewhat unique for its length. All known versions are long, some running to twenty-nine stanzas. It is a purely local ballad, its popularity being confined to the Upper Cumberland region of Tennessee where the incident happened. The ballad lyrics force "truth" to conform to ballad conventions. Thus, in the song both Teek and Joe admit their guilt because it is commonplace in murderer's farewell ballads to do so. In actuality, of course, only Joe confessed to the crime. Moreover, as is common in many American ballads, the desire for money and whiskey is suggested as the real culprit; in other words the murderers are not really responsible for their acts. The moralistic ending and the request that parents, sister, and brothers understand are also typical in native American ballads.

The present text was contributed "several years ago" to the Tennessee Folklore Society by a D.P. Glenn whose residence is not specified. The melody line is from a version recorded by Jessie Hudelston (1925–1979) in 1976, Cookeville, Tennessee. The tune is essentially that of "Life's Railway to Heaven" (perhaps better known as "Life Is Like a Mountain Railway"), a melody written by gospel songwriter Charlie D. Tillman (1861–1943) in 1890. This fact suggests that the ballad was either written more than a decade after the events it describes or, more likely, that it originally had another melody.

The Isbell mentioned here was William Isbell, tax assessor, who was the Braswells' intended victim (the murders occurred in his home). Campbell Bohannon was the sheriff at the time of the hangings and McFerrin was a Methodist minister who, along with two other preachers, was with the Braswells the night before their hanging.

Behind the Great Wall

COLLECTED MARCH 21, 1951 BY IRENE J. CARLISLE FROM LEWIS BEDINGFIELD,
SPRINGDALE, ARKANSAS. TRANSCRIPTION BY MRS. HOWARD R. CLARK.

Cass County's a great county,
Where I first saw the light;
Brought up by fond parents
In the pathway of right.
I was left an orphan
At the age of ten years.
At the grave of my mother
I shed many tears.

Texarkana is a little city
Where I first met my fate;
I was arrested for forgery
While walkin' the street;
The charge it was forgery,
The crime it was small;
They said this would put me
Behind the Great Wall.

One mornin' in the courtroom,
Downhearted and sad,
Pleadin' for mercy;
No mercy they had.
The verdict was read;
'Twas bitter as gall:
Two years at hard labor,
Behind the Great Wall.

One morning I 'as handcuffed
And taken to the pen;
I arrived about midday
With a few other men.
The gates were thrown open,
And I walked through the hall,
And I knew I 'as a convict
Behind the Great Wall.

Next morning I 'as assigned
To Imperial Number One;
I then knew
My work had begun.
They gave me an axe,
A wedge and a maul;
Said, "You'll be a woodcutter
Behind the Great Wall."

Come, all you young fellows;
Take warning from me;
You lose your best life, boys,
When you lose your liberty.
Perhaps you've a mother
Who'll mourn your downfall;
But you're dead to the world, boys,
Behind the Great Wall.

This song is generally recalled today because of a May 5, 1935 recording by the original Carter Family (A.P. [1891–1960], Sara [1898–1979], and Maybelle [1908–1978]) under the title "Behind Those Stone Walls." The song, however, predated the Carter recording as the present text indicates. It was collected by Irene J. Carlisle on March 21, 1951 from Lewis Bedingfield of Springdale, Arkansas. At the time Bedingfield was about thirty-eight years old and operated a shoe-repair shop in Springdale. He was born in New Boston, Texas and learned this ballad from a prisoner in the local jail. This was probably before 1926 because about that year Bedingfield left home to work in Oklahoma. In 1931 he moved to Arkansas where he lived for at least the next twenty years. Carlisle described Bedingfield as "somewhat shy" but handsome and affable, with a pleasant singing voice.

Bedingfield's text differs from most versions, including the Carter Family's, by having the protagonist hailing from Cass County, Texas rather than St. Louis. He generally meets his fate in New York; the reference to Imperial no. 1 is also unique to Bedingfield's version. There are some other minor word differences and the tune itself varies slightly from the usual melody. Besides the titles used by Bedingfield and the Carters, the song is also known as "Saint Louis, Bright City," under which title it was collected by Vance Randolph, December 9, 1941. His informant, Wythe Bishop of Fayetteville, Arkansas, said he learned it in the late '80s or early '90s and it is possible that this ballad was written in the latter half of the nineteenth century. It is almost certain, though, that it is based on even older models.

G. Malcolm Laws's contention (*Native American Balladry*, p. 266) that this is of doubtful currency in tradition can be discounted. I personally have heard it from traditional singers several times in the past ten years, most of their versions coming directly or indirectly from the Carter Family recording. According to Bedingfield, the young man he learned the song from frequently entertained crowds outside the jail by singing this, and other songs, in exchange for cigarettes.

Charles Guiteau

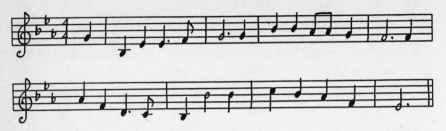

COLLECTED BY BYRON ARNOLD FROM CORIE LAMBERT, MOBILE, ALABAMA, PROBABLY
1947. TRANSCRIPTION BY BYRON ARNOLD.

My name is Charles Guiteau,
My name I'll never deny;
I leave my aged parents
In sorrow for to die.

But little did I think
While in my youthful bloom
That I'd be taken to the scaffold
To meet my fatal doom.

Down at the old depot
I tried to escape,
But providence being against me
I found it was too late.

Judge Clark, he read the sentence,
The clerk he wrote it by:
"For the murder of James A. Garfield
You are condemned to die."

My sister came to the prison
To bid me a last farewell;
She threw her arms around me
And wept so bitterly.

She said, "My darling brother,
This day you are to die
For the murder of James A. Garfield
Upon the scaffold high."

The hangman is awaiting,
It's a quarter after three;
The black cap's on my forehead
I never more can see.

But when I'm dead and buried
Oh, Lord, remember me.

COLLECTED IN 1977 BY BURT FEINTUCH FROM CLORINE LAWSON, NOBOB, KENTUCKY.
TRANSCRIPTION BY DREW BEISSWENGER.

Come all you young people and listen unto me,
And likewise pay attention to these few words I say.
For the murder of James A. Garfield, I am condemned to die,
On the thirtieth day of June, upon a scaffold high.

CHORUS:
My name is Charles Guiteau, that name I'll never deny.
I left my aged parents in sorrow for to die.
How little did I think, while in my youthful bloom,
That I'd be taken to the scaffold to meet my fatal doom.

'Twas down at the depot I tried to make my escape.
But, Providence against me, I found I was too late.
I tried to play insane; I found that would not do.
The people were against me, proved I was untrue.

CHORUS: (same as before)

My sister came to prison to bid her last farewell.
She threw her arms around me and wept most bitter and well.
She says, "My darling brother, tomorrow you must die,
For the murder of James A. Garfield, upon the scaffold high."

CHORUS: (same as before)

James A. Garfield of Ohio was a dark-horse candidate who became the compromise Republican presidential nominee in 1880 after supporters of U.S. Grant and James G. Blaine could not agree. A member of the liberal faction of the party, Garfield defeated the Democratic candidate, Winfield S. Hancock, for the presidency. Garfield attacked the then firmly entrenched spoils system and was, apparently, making significant changes in this regard when on July 2, 1881, after only four months in office, he was shot while waiting in the Baltimore and Potomac railway station in Washington. He lingered on for over two-and-a-half months, finally succumbing on September 19. In the meantime, his assassin, a disappointed office-seeker named Charles Guiteau, was apprehended and indicted for murder. At his trial, Guiteau pleaded insanity but was found guilty and hanged on June 30, 1882. This ballad, purporting to be Guiteau's own work, soon came to be widely known and is still popular with traditional singers.

"Charles Guiteau" is based on an earlier murder ballad, *Lament of James Rodgers,* Who Was Executed November 12th, 1858, for the Murder of Mr. Swanston" which was attributed to a J.A.D. and set to the tune of "Home, Sweet Home." The original publication was only four stanzas but a subsequent broadside of the Rodgers song expanded it to thirteen stanzas. Some of the lyrics from this ballad were adopted for "Charles Guiteau" but the melody used by J.A.D. was not utilized.

The first of the two texts given here was collected by Byron Arnold from Corie Lambert, Mobile, Alabama, at an unspecified date but probably in 1947. Lambert, a native of Georgia who came to Alabama when she was only six months old, was one of Arnold's primary informants. Most of her songs were learned from her grandmother and seem to be examples of "memory culture" for Arnold notes that she had not sung many of them for a long time. The second text was collected by Bert Feintuch from Clorine Lawson, Nobob, Kentucky, in 1977. Mrs. Lawson was born in 1917 near her present home but spent part of her life in Indiana and Florida where she worked as a nurse, her present occupation. She learned most of her songs from her mother, Ina Norman Jones, and usually sings them while working. For years she has also sung her ballads and folksongs to her children. Mrs. Lawson has been recorded a number of times by collectors connected with Western Kentucky University in Bowling Green, her first contributions dating from the late 1950s.

Jesse James

COLLECTED FROM ROBERT SHIFLETT, BROWN'S COVE, VIRGINIA, 1962 BY GEORGE
FOSS.   TRANSCRIPTION BY GEORGE FOSS.

Living in Missouri was a brave bold man,
Known from Seattle, Washington to Birmingham,
From Boston, Massachusetts across the states,
From Denver, Colorado to the Golden Gate.

Sitting in the saddle he won his fame,
Every nook and corner knew of Jesse James.
Perhaps you read about him in your homes at night,
And if the wind blew down the chimney you would shake with fright.

Jesse said "Some more coin we need."
He oiled up his rifle, got his trusty steed.
Galloped over to his brother Frank,
Says, "We'll have to have some money from the Pettsville bank."

He rode into town about ten o'clock.
The cashier and the banker 'ceived a terrible shock.
While Jesse kept him covered with his forty-four,
His pals got a half a million dollars or more.

Jesse was sitting in his home alone;
His wife had left him there to straighten out the home.
He was sitting in the kitchen when the doorbell rang.
In stepped Ford, a member of the outlaw gang.

Ford said, "Tonight we will make a haul."
Jesse's wife's picture was hanging on the wall.
The western mail ran through the town,
Jesse reached for his rifle, knocked the picture down.

Jesse said to Ford, "I will hang it back up there."
He picked up the picture, climbed upon a chair.
Ford aimed the forty-four at Jesse's head,
And news rang around the world that Jesse James was dead.

Next week on his tombstone, these words they ran:
"If you're going to live a bandit live a single man."
For perhaps Jesse James wouldn't have lost his life
Hadn't been for the picture of his darling wife.

Jesse James

WORDS BY ROGER LEWIS   MUSIC BY F. HENRI KLICKMANN

Although the musical notation contains numerous errors, it appears here as originally published.

> Living in Missouri was a bold, bad man,
> Was known from Seattle down to Birmingham;
> From Boston, Massachusetts, right across the States,
> To Denver, Colorado, and the Golden Gates.
> The people will forget a lot of famous names,
> But ev'ry nook and corner knows of Jesse James.
> We used to read about him in our home at night,
> When the wind blew down the chimney we would shake with fright.

CHORUS:
Jesse James! We used to read about him,
Jesse James! In our home at night;
Jesse James! We used to read about him,
When the wind blew down the chimney we would shake with fright.
(Entire chorus is repeated)

Jesse said one evening, "Boys, some coin we need,"
He polished up his rifle, got his trusty steed;
And then he galloped over to his brother Frank,
Said, "We've got to get some money from the Pittsfield Bank."
They got in town next morning, it was ten o'clock,
The cashier at the bank he got an awful shock,
While Jesse had him covered with his forty-four,
His pals took out a half a million bones or more.

CHORUS:
Jesse James! He had the cashier covered,
Jesse James! With his forty-four;
Jesse James! He had the cashier covered
And his pals took out a half a million bones or more.
(Entire chorus is repeated)

Jesse was in his cabin one day all alone,
His wife had left him there to straighten up the home,
Was scrubbing out the kitchen when the doorbell rang,
And in walked Ford, a member of the outlaw gang.
A photograph of Jesse's wife was on the wall,
When Jesse said to Ford, "Tonight we'll make a haul,
At ten o'clock the western mail will come thro' town,"
He turned to get his rifle, knocked the picture down.

CHORUS:
Jesse James! He turned to get his rifle,
Jesse James! Hanging on the wall;
Jesse James! He turned to get his rifle,
Yes, he turned to get his rifle hanging on the wall.
(Entire chorus is repeated)

Jesse said, "I'll hang the picture back up there,"
He stooped and picked it up and stood upon a chair;
And Ford then aimed his forty-four at Jesse's head,
And news spread round the country Jesse James was dead.
So next week on his tombstone were some lines that ran,
"If you want to be a bandit stay a single man,
For we know that Jesse never would have lost his life,
If it wasn't for that darn old picture of his wife."

CHORUS:
Jesse James! He tried to hang the picture,
Jesse James! Picture of his wife;
Jesse James! He tried to hang the picture,
Yes, he tried to hang the picture and he lost his life.
(Entire chorus is repeated)

This ballad was probably written by F. Henri Klickmann and Roger Lewis; at least Klickmann copyrighted it on April 3, 1911 although he did not publish it at the time. Little more than a month later, on May 15, music publisher Will Rossiter copyrighted the same version. Both the composer and lyricist were very active in the popular music scene of the day. Klickmann, a Chicago native, collaborated frequently with Lewis and some of the most important pop song lyricists of his time, including Andy Razaf, Bob Miller, and Al Dubin. Probably his best known composition was "Floating Down to Cotton Town." Lewis (1885–1948), a native of Colfax, Illinois, is best remembered for "Oceana Roll" and the novelty number "Down By the Winegar Woiks." There seems little reason to doubt that Klickmann and Lewis were responsible for this "Jesse James" ballad, especially since there is no prior claim. There is always the possibility suggested by Norm Cohen, p. 107, that the two were merely cashing in on an already existing parody. Since there is no evidence of such a parody before 1911, Klickmann and Lewis's claim seems irrefutable.

There has, of course, been a longstanding interest in Jesse Woodson James (1847–1882). Legends about his life and crimes are, in most cases, more interesting than what really happened. Neither the first train or bank robber, although he has sometimes been credited as such, James had a criminal career that lasted from February 13, 1866, when he participated in a bank robbery in Liberty, Missouri, until his assassination on April 3, 1882. Even before his death, James was being made out a hero by many and the manner of his death (he was shot in the back by a cousin) accelerated the process. Some rather sensational pamphlets recounted his supposed exploits, and several plays, and later movies, about the outlaw were produced. There were also a number of ballads about James, at least two of which entered folk tradition. One, first published in 1887, harped on James's death at the hands of "that dirty little coward" (Robert Ford) while the second one, the Klickmann–Lewis effort, took a more humorous approach. In 1911 a play, *The James Boys in Missouri,* was successfully revived in St. Louis and a movie, *Jesse James,* was also released, two events that may have occasioned the writing of the new ballad. This "Jesse James" ballad fits the "Casey Jones" tune and has occasionally been collected with that melody but it was not originally composed to it. For the sake of comparison the Klickmann–Lewis text and tune are provided above with the traditional version. The anti-marriage quip in the last verse of this song is perhaps its most unique feature.

The traditional text was collected in 1962 by George Foss from Robert Shiflett, Brown's Cove, Virginia. For more information about Shiflett see the notes to "Texas Rangers."

Stagalee

COLLECTED BY RUBY PICKENS TARTT FROM VERA HALL, LIVINGSTON, ALABAMA, JUNE 17, 1947. TRANSCRIPTION BY BYRON ARNOLD.

Bad man Stagalee when he bad,
He bad wid a gun
Stagalee, Stagalee—you must-a been a sinner
Ev'ry Christmas eve they give Stagalee a dinner
Bad man Stagalee, when he bad
He bad wid a gun.

Don't you remember you remember
One dark stormy night
Stagalee and Bill O. Lion
Dey had dat noble fight.

Bill O. Lion tole Stagalee
Please don't take my life
I got three little children
And a dear lil' lovin' wife

Stagalee told Billy O. Lion
I don't care for your three lil' children
Or even your lovin' wife
You stole mah Stetson hat
And I'm goin to take yo' life

Stagalee pulled out his forty-four
It went boom boom boom
It wasn't long 'fore Bill O. Lion
Were layin' on de flo'.

Stagalee's woman she went to her boss
Said, "Please give me some change.
Dey got my baby in de station house
An' mah business mus' be 'ranged."

Stagalee asked his woman
"How much change has you got?"
She run her han' in her stocking feet
And pulled out a hundred spot.
She had to get mo' money.

Most of the singers who include this ballad in their repertoire are of the opinion that it refers to an actual person but who that original was, even whether he was black or white, is in dispute. Some say that he was Jim Stack Lee, the black son of Stack Lee, a Confederate cavalryman who fathered many interracial babies. There is no question that Jim Stack Lee was a much feared bully and murderer, but whether he is the prototype for Stagolee is unclear. Some believe that the bad man was a deck-worker named after the steamboat *Stack-o-Lee.* There are possibly other claimants but, at this late date, it is unlikely that any one of them can be definitely proven to be the original. It is even less likely that the exact place of his exploits can be determined although most speculations on the subject suggest that they happened either in Memphis or St. Louis. Much has been made of the fact that the Lee family in Memphis owned a steamboat called the *Stacker Lee* which operated on the Mississippi. Less often noted is that Jim Lee, owner of this steamboat, had a son also named Stacker Lee.

Whoever Stagolee was and whenever the song about him originated, the ballad was in circulation by the 1890s. Charles Haffer of Coahoma County, Mississippi, an informant for the Library of Congress Archive of Folk Song, remembered singing about Stagolee's exploits in 1895, while Will Starks, also a Mississippi Delta resident taped by the Archive of Folk Song, first heard "Stagolee" in 1897 from a man who had learned it sometime earlier in labor camps near St. Louis. By the first decade of the twentieth century it was commonly sung throughout much of the South and was "being sung by the Negro vagrants all over the country." In the intervening years the bad man's popularity has hardly waned. He is still the hero of toasts, songs, and tales found not only in the South but in black communities in Michigan, Pennsylvania, New York, and Illinois as well. In 1958 pop singer Lloyd Price recorded a version of "Stagger Lee" that became number 1 on *Billboard's* Hot 100 and remained on the chart for at least fifteen weeks.* Undoubtedly, one of the reasons for Stagolee's popularity in black communities is that he is a Negro who flouts the conventions of white society and gets away with it, or seems to.

Stagolee is known by various other related names including Stackolee, Stackerlee, Stackalee, Stacker Lee, and Staggerlee. Versions of the song about him have been collected in Texas, Alabama, Kentucky, Arkansas, Florida, Louisiana, Mississippi, and Tennessee. The central event in every version is a gun battle between Stagolee and Billy, or Bully, Lyons or, as in the present text, Bill O. Lion, resulting from Stagolee's anger at losing his Stetson hat while gambling. Billy is soon bested and begs for mercy but Stagolee responds with a complete lack of compassion. In most versions Stagolee is captured and ends his life in prison or is killed and goes to Hell. The present text, however, makes no mention of his subsequent fate but in every other respect is a typical set of lyrics about the most important and longest-lived bad man in black lore.

The present version was collected June 17, 1947 by Ruby Pickens Tartt from Vera Hall, Livingston, Alabama. Tartt (1880–1974) was an amateur folklorist who spent much of her ninety-four years collecting folksongs from rural blacks in her native Sumter County, Alabama. Virginia Pounds Brown and Laurella Owens have produced a book, *Toting the Lead Row: Ruby Pickens Tartt, Alabama Folklorist* (University, Alabama: The University of Alabama Press, 1981), that discusses Tartt's life, collections, and several of the informants she recorded material from. One of the most famous of these was Vera Hall (1906–1964) who is best remembered today for her recording of the song "Another Man Done Gone" which was published in John and Alan Lomax's book, *Best Loved American Folk Songs* (1947). Hall was also well-known for her spirituals which were featured on several nationwide programs. Much of her life story is given in Alan Lomax's volume *The Rainbow Sign* (1959). Hall spent most of her life working as a domestic servant in Livingston and Tuscaloosa. It was in the latter city that she died.

---

*There are conflicting accounts of how long Price's version was on the charts. According to Joel Whitburn's *Top Pop Records 1955–1970* (Detroit: Gale Research Company, 1972), no page numbers given, it was on the charts for twenty-one weeks. But in the same author's *The Billboard Book of Top 40 Hits: 1955 to Present* (New York: Billboard Publications, Inc., 1983), p. 220, it only appeared for fifteen weeks.

Ballads of Family Opposition to Lovers

Charming Beauty Bright

COLLECTED BY GEORGE FOSS FROM MARYBIRD McALLISTER, BROWN'S COVE, VIRGINIA, 1961. TRANSCRIPTION BY GEORGE FOSS.

Once I courted a fair and beauty bright,
I courted her by day and I courted her by night.
I courted her for love and love I did intend.
I'm sure she never had any right to complain.

When her cruel old parents came this to know,
That I was a-courting his daughter also,
He locked her up so high and he treated her so 'vere [severe]
I never, never more got the sight of my dear.

Then to the war I thought I would go,
To see what I would forget my love or no,
Oh when I did get there the army shined so bright
It put me in fresh remembrance of my own heart's delight.

Sevent long years I served as a king,
Oh sevent long years I 'turned home again,
With my heart full of war and my eyes full of tears,
But I never, never more got the sight of my dear.

Then her cruel old parents I thought it I would go,
To see what I could see my love or no,
Her mother saw me coming, she wringed her hands and cried,
"My daughter loved you dearly and for your sake she died."

Then I was struck like one had been slain,
The tears from my eyes like showers of rain,
This crying lordy mercy this pain I cannot bear,
My true love is gone and I wish that I was there.

This ballad most likely originated as a British broadside but, if so, the original remains unknown. In any case, it is more popular in the United States than in its probable homeland. It has been collected primarily in the South but has also been found in Kansas, Indiana, Ohio, Illinois, Massachusetts, Vermont, Wisconsin, and Missouri. The ballad is known traditionally under various titles including, in addition to the one given here, "Beauty, Beauty Bright," "The Lover's Lament," "The First Girl I Courted," and "Seven Year Song." Textually, most versions are very similar although some include the detail that the narrator goes mad and is sent to a mental institution.

The present text was collected in 1961 by George Foss from Marybird McAllister, Brown's Cove, Virginia. McAllister was an illiterate singer with a large repertoire that included several unusual versions of widely known ballads. Her specific sources of songs are not given, but she probably learned many of them from other members of her community which, at the time of collection, had a strong folksinging tradition.

The Drowsy Sleeper

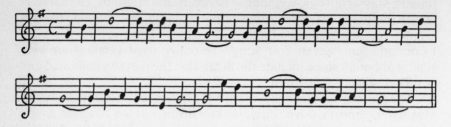

COLLECTED BY CHARLES W. JOYNER FROM EVA ESDORN, MURRELLS INLET, SOUTH CAROLINA, AUGUST, 1969. TRANSCRIPTION BY CHARLES W. JOYNER.

Who is at my bedroom window?
Who is that this time of night?
It is I your old true lover
Weeping under the willow tree.

Mary, Mary go and ask your mother
If she'll consent you to be my wife.
If she says no come quickly and tell me
This night no longer I'll bother thee.

It is no use to ask my mother
For she intends to keep me free.
So, Willie dear go and court some other
Another girl you'll love like me.

I can court some other fair girl,
I can climb the tallest trees.
But, Mary dear, there's none I love,
There's none I love as well as thee.

Mary, Mary go and ask your father
If he'll consent you to be my bride.
If he says no come quickly and tell me,
This night no longer I'll bother thee.

It is no use to ask my father
For he intends to keep me free.
So, Willie dear, please leave me forever
For there's none I love as well as thee.

Willie pulled out his golden dagger,
Stabbed it through his aching heart.
Goodbye Mary, goodbye darling,
I am now at rest with thee.

72

Mary picked up her golden dagger,
Stabbed it through her milk-white breast.
Goodbye Mama, Goodbye Daddy,
I and Willie are now at rest.

This ballad is frequently confused with "The Silver Dagger," a similar ballad of American origin. It is generally accepted that "The Drowsy Sleeper" originated as a British broadside ballad. It concerns a visit between a lover and his mistress at her window in which he is trying to get her to ask her parents for consent to their love. She says it will be unavailing and, in some texts, adds an implication that he has been making love to another. After this exchange he leaves feeling disconsolate. This basic story has undergone several modifications; in America "The Silver Dagger" is frequently used for a conclusion.

Although it is unclear from the present texts, this ballad refers to an ancient pagan custom that was once widespread throughout Western Europe. At one time it was accepted practice for a couple to spend a night together prior to marriage. This custom, called the Night Visit, was the topic of songs as early as the sixteenth century. Typically, these Night Visit songs included the following episodes: (1) the youth's arrival at his fiancee's home; (2) his tapping at the window to gain admittance; (3) her refusal, because of her parents' presence; (4) his threatening to leave; and (5) her giving in to his request when she realizes that otherwise she may lose him. Not all of these details appear in every Night Visit song but they do reflect the actual customary practice. What parental opposition existed was only token, for in reality, they endorsed the custom despite the Church's strong opposition to the practice.

A similar ballad, "The Silver Dagger," is generally assumed to be of American origin but, according to Cecil Sharp (II, p. 229), it takes its title and some of its details from a British ballad. There is no doubt that the conclusion of "The Silver Dagger," in which the couple usually dies, is frequently borrowed for "The Drowsy Sleeper." That is the case with the present version.

The present text was collected in August, 1969 by Charles W. Joyner from Eva Esdorn, Murrells Inlet, South Carolina. Esdorn's source is unknown.

Rainbow Willow

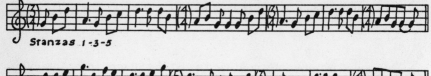

Stanzas 1-3-5

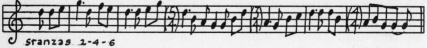

Stanzas 2-4-6

COLLECTED BY GEORGE FOSS FROM VIOLA COLE, FANCY GAP, VIRGINIA, 1962.
TRANSCRIPTION BY GEORGE FOSS.

Last night I dreamed of my true love
All in my arms I had her;
When I awoke there was no such there
I was forced to lie without her.

Her yeller hair like links of gold
Were dangling over my pillow;
She is the darling of my heart,
She is the rainbow willow.

I went into her uncle's house
Inquiring for my sweet one.
They answered me, the're no such there
She's in another toom, sir.

But locks and bars to flender [splinters] fly,
And quickly I got to her.
I took her on and I followed on
And after us did follow.

Her uncle and another man
All after us did follow.
They swore before I returned home
All in my blood they'd waller.

There was blood spilled on ever' side
I drew my love from amongst them;
And if you want to gain your love,
Just fight and overcome them.

I Dreamt Last Night of My True Love

COLLECTED BY MERCEDES STEELY FROM MRS. NORA JOHNSON, EBENEZER, NORTH CAROLINA, APRIL, 1935. TRANSCRIPTION BY MERCEDES STEELY AND JAN PHILIP SCHINHAN.

I dreamt last night of my true love,
All in my arms I had her,
But when I woke it was not so;
I was forced to leave without her.

Her long yellow hair like strands of gold
Hang dangling around my pillow,
For the only girl I have ever loved,
I will follow the railroads after her.

I went into her uncle's house,
Inquiring for my lover;
The answer they give, there is none such here,
For neither would I keep her.

In hearing of her true love's voice
She come creeping to the window:
"I'd freely be with you, my love,
But locks and bolts do hinder."

He stood right still all in a maze,
A-studying how to gain 'er;
His passions rose, he drew his sword
And smashed through doors and winders.

He taken his true love by 'er lily-white hand
And his broad wide sword in the other:
"If any man loves her better'n I do,
In 'is own heart's blood he shall waller;
If any man loves her better'n I do,
Let one man fight another."

Fight on, fight on, my brave young son,
You are fighting for your lover,
And oh, to show, to let the old folks know
Young men will have thy daughters.

This ballad is usually known as "Locks and Bolts" or "I Dreamed of My True Love." Widely collected in the American South, the song is also known in Missouri, Indiana, Oklahoma, and Wisconsin and, most likely, is known in other places where it has not been reported by folksong collectors. Possibly it is derived from a Scottish song known as "The Lass O' Bennochie" but Paul G. Brewster and G. Malcolm Laws are of the opinion that it is descended from a broadside ballad of 1631, "A Constant Wife," which is found in Hyder E. Rollins' edition of *The Pepys Ballads* (Cambridge: Harvard University Press, 1929), p. 201. Whatever the circumstances of its origin it certainly is one of the most popular traditional ballads in America dealing with family opposition to lovers. G. Malcolm Laws lists it in *American Balladry from British Broadsides* as M13.

The first version printed here was collected July 10, 1962 by George Foss from Viola Cole of Fancy Gap, Virginia. Textually, Cole's version is typical of most American versions of the ballad in that the lovers triumph over their opposition. Melodically, however, Cole's version seems to be different, being set at a higher pitch than most and varying the meter from 3/4 to 4/4. Perhaps, though, it is not quite fair to make such judgments because most reported examples have not included accompanying musical transcriptions.

The second version was collected in April, 1935 by Mercedes Steely from Mrs. Nora Johnson, Ebenezer, North Carolina. Mrs. Johnson's source for the ballad is not mentioned but she did have a large repertoire that she contributed to Steely's collection. Most of the other songs she knew were learned from various members of her family, and it seems likely they were also her source for "I Dreamt Last Night of My True Love."

Ballads of Lovers' Disguises and Tricks

Little Willie and Mary

COLLECTED BY THEODORE GARRISON FROM MRS. SYBIL FREEMAN, MARSHALL, ARKANSAS, APRIL, 1941. TRANSCRIPTION BY THEODORE GARRISON.

Little Willie and Mary stood on the seashore
Their last farewell to take;
She says, "Little Willie, if I see you no more,
Oh, surely my heart it will break."
"Oh, be not dismayed, Little Mary," he said,
As he kissed the young girl by his side,
"As sure as I live, I'll truly return
And make Little Mary my bride."

Three years had gone by and no news had come.
One day Mary stood in her door;
A beggar passed by with a patch on his eye
And his jacket all ragged and tore.
"Have pity on me; your friend I will be,
Your fortune I'll tell you beside.
The one that you mourn will never return
To make Little Mary his bride."

She trembled and staggered and hastily did say,
"All money I have I will give,
If the question I ask you you tell me true,
Oh say, does my Willie live?"
"He lives it is true, in poverty, too;
Shipwrecked and misfortuned beside.
He'll never return, for he is too poor
To make Little Mary his bride."

"No one knows the joy I feel,
Although his misfortune I mourn;
He's welcome to me, though in poverty he be
With his jacket all ragged and torn."
The beggar then tore the patch from his eye,
His jacket lay down by his side,
Coat, vest, and trousers; with cheeks red as a rose
Little Willie stood by Mary's side.

"Forgive me, dear Mary; forgive me, I pray.
It was only your love that I tried."
They hastened away at the close of the day,
And he made Little Mary his bride.

This ballad is generally known by the present title, as "Mary and Willie," "Willie and Mary," "Little Mary, the Sailor's Bride," and "The Single Sailor." It originated as a broadside ballad in early nineteenth century England, being issued by such broadside publishers as Such, Catnach, Evans, and Jackson. English collector William Alexander Barrett included a composite text in his *English Folk-Songs* (1891), parts of it from singers in Bedfordshire and Cheshire. In America it has been reported as traditional song from Missouri, Michigan, Montana, Maine, Vermont, Massachusetts, Indiana, Tennessee, and Mississippi.

"Little Willie and Mary" belongs to a large body of traditional balladry, most of if dating from nineteenth century broadsides, that deal with lovers' disguises and tricks. In most of these the lover in disguise tells the girl that her sweetheart has died, using this means and his disguise to test her faithfulness. These are frequently called "broken token ballads" because the disguised lover reveals his identity by producing half of a broken token that he and his sweetheart shared. In none of these songs is the lover recognized until he removes his disguise or otherwise reveals himself, a circumstance that goes against all logic because the two usually have been parted only a relatively short time, often three or seven years. On the other hand, it is hardly more illogical than the rest of these ballads which are based on the great improbability that a man long separated from his sweetheart would act in the manner described here. This is an instance where romantic sentimentality dominates logic in maintaining such songs in an active folk tradition.

The present version was collected April, 1941 by Theodore Garrison from Mrs. Sybil Freeman, Marshall, Arkansas. Mrs. Freeman, who was about forty-five years old at the time of collection, was the wife of a country storekeeper in Searcy County, Arkansas. There is no indication who she learned the ballad from but the text is unusual in that the last stanza has only four lines rather than eight. This shortened final stanza presents no problems melodically, for lines three and four are sung to exactly the same music as lines seven and eight.

Miss Mary Belle

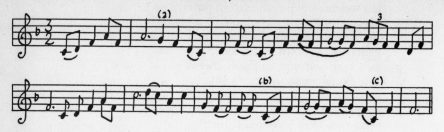

COLLECTED BY ANNABEL MORRIS BUCHANAN FROM MRS. CARRIE LOUISE BECK, HENDERSONVILLE, NORTH CAROLINA, JULY 22, 1954. TRANSCRIPTION BY ANNABEL MORRIS BUCHANAN.

Miss Mary Belle strolled through her garden
Alone, all on one summer day,
There a soldier came and walked beside her,
In a manner bold, these words did say.

"Miss Mary Belle, go ask your mother
If you may be a bride of mine;
If she says yes, come back and tell me,
If she says no, we will run away."

"Oh, no, kind sir, you're a man of honor,
A man of honor you may be,
But to ask a broken-hearted maiden
A stranger's wife this day to be.

"I have a true love across the ocean,
It's been seven long years since his face I've seen,
But if he stays there seven years longer,
No man on earth shall marry me."

"Prehaps he's on the deep sea drownded,
Prehaps he's on some battlefield slain,
Prehaps he's gone and wed another,
And forgotten thee, who waits in vain."

"If he's drownded, I hope he's happy,
Or if he's on some battlefield slain;
Or if he's gone and wed another,
I'll love the girl that wears his name."

He took his hands out of his pockets,
His fingers both were slim and small;
Upon them he wore an engagement ring,
And at his feet Mary Belle did fall.

He picked her up all in his bosom,
The kisses he gave her was one, two, three;
"Wake up, Mary Belle, wake up, my darling,
This day I've come to marry thee."

Perhaps the quintessential "broken token ballad" (see discussion of such ballads in the notes for "Little Willie and Mary") is this item usually called "Pretty Fair Maid" or "Pretty Fair Maid in the Garden." It is also known traditionally by several other titles including "The Broken Token," "The Maiden in the Garden," "The Single Sailor," "The Returning Soldier," "The Rugged Soldier," "Edward," "A Sailor's Sweetheart," "Seven Long Years He Has Kept Me Waiting," "The Test of Love," and "A Sweetheart in the Army." It originated in the early nineteenth century as an English broadside titled "The Sailor's Return" and it remains quite popular with traditional singers. Versions have been reported from Missouri, Virginia, North Carolina, West Virginia, Ohio, Tennessee, Georgia, Kentucky, Florida, Texas, Massachusetts, and Nova Scotia. Some of its popularity with American singers can be traced to mass media influences, in particular a recording by Kentucky country artist Cousin Emmy (Cynthia May Carver) (1903–1980).

The present text was collected July 22, 1954 by Annabel Morris Buchanan from Mrs. Carrie Louise Beck, Hendersonville, North Carolina. For more information about Buchanan see the notes to "The False Knight Upon the Road." Beck learned the ballad in childhood from her mother, Mrs. Evelyn Roberson Thames, Manning, South Carolina, and from her paternal grandmother, Mrs. Louise Thames. As with most other texts of this particular ballad, the token is not actually broken but, rather, an engagement ring.

Young John Riley

COLLECTED IN 1977 BY BURT FEINTUCH FROM STREET BUTLER, ELKTON, KENTUCKY.
TRANSCRIPTION BY DREW BEISSWENGER.

As I walked out one morning early,
All for the health of the fresh air,
I chanced to spy a lovely creature,
Who seemed to me like a lily fair.

So quickly I stepped up and asked her,
If she would be a sailor's wife.
"Oh no, kind sir, to tell you plainly,
I prefer sweet single life."

"Oh dear, what is the reason
That you differ from the female kind?
You are beautiful, both young and handsome,
And from man you do decline."

"Seven years ago I promised to marry.
Seven long years he's been gone from me.
I promised to marry young John Riley,
Who's been the cause of my sadness here."

"Don't wait on young Riley longer.
Come go with me to some foreign shore.
We'll sail away to Pennsylvania
And there live forever more."

"I won't go to Pennsylvania,
Nor will I go to some foreign shore.
My heart is with him, I can't forget him,
Although his face I may see no more.

"Seven long years he's been gone from me;
In seven more he may return.
Seven long years he's been gone from me;
Seven more I'll wait for him."

So quickly I stepped up and embraced her.
The kisses I gave were two or three,
Saying, "I am the man you call John Riley.
I've come home to marry you.

"I sailed the world all in commotion;
Money I have laid up in store.
I'll no longer tarry, but soon we'll marry,
And I will leave thee never more."

There are two broadside ballads named "John Riley" commonly found in American tradition and they both deal with lovers' disguises and tricks. This is the one G. Malcolm Laws lists as N37 in his *American Balladry From British Broadsides*. It is distinguished from the other "John Riley" primarily by the suggestion of the trip to Pennsylvania, the man's accumulation of wealth during the time he and his sweetheart have been apart, and the proposal of marriage. The ballad is usually known as "John Riley" but also is found traditionally as "George Riley" or "Young Riley" or with some variant spelling of the last name. Most likely the song is derived from an eighteenth century ballad, "The Constant Damsel," which appeared in a Dublin songbook published in 1791.

"John Riley" has been collected primarily in the South, versions being reported from Virginia, West Virginia, Kentucky, North Carolina, and Tennessee. It has also been reported in ballad collections from Missouri, Ohio, Indiana, Michigan, and Vermont but its primary habitat seems to be the southern Appalachians. The present version was collected in 1977 by Burt Feintuch from Street Butler, Elkton, Kentucky. Butler (1904–1977), who spent nearly three decades working in other states, thought of himself primarily as a Todd County, Kentucky farmer. He was an outstanding source of information on the area's history and music and possessed a large number of stories about the titles of tunes he played on the fiddle. Among the unusual instrumentals he knew was a piece called "Higgins' Farewell" that he connected with an incident in which a local fiddler named Jim Higgins was shot and killed. Butler learned most of his songs from his mother who, most likely, was his source for "Young John Riley."

Ballads of Faithful Lovers

Jimmy Loud

COLLECTED BY MERCEDES STEELY FROM MRS. NORA JOHNSON, EBENEZER, NORTH CAROLINA, APRIL, 1935. TRANSCRIPTION BY MERCEDES STEELY.

"Jimmy Loud, Jimmy Loud, Jimmy Loud," he cried,
"Pray hold your hands for a while,
I think I see my father a-coming;
He is riding so many miles.

"Oh, have you brought me gold, dear father,
Or have you bought me free,
Or have you come for to see me hang
All under this gallows tree?"

"I've neither brought you gold, my son,
Nor I've neither bought you free,
But I have come for to see you hang
All under this gallows tree."

"Jimmy Loud, Jimmy Loud, Jimmy Loud," he cries,
"Pray hold your hands for a while,
I think I see my mother a-coming;
She is riding so many miles.

"Oh, have you brought me gold, dear mother,
Or have you bought me free,
Or have you come for to see me hang
All under this gallows tree?"

"I've neither brought you gold, my son,
Nor I've neither bought you free,
But I have come for to see you hang
All under this gallows tree."

"Jimmy Loud, Jimmy Loud, Jimmy Loud," he cries,
"Pray hold your hands for a while,
I think I see my brother a-coming;
He is riding so many miles.

"Oh, have you brought me gold, dear brother,
Or have you bought me free,
Or have you come for to see me hang
All under this gallows tree?"

"I've neither brought you gold, my brother,
Nor I've neither bought you free,
But I have come for to see you hang
All under this gallows tree."

"Jimmy Loud, Jimmy Loud, Jimmy Loud," he cries,
"Pray hold your hands for a while,
I think I see my sister a-coming;
She is riding so many miles.

"Oh, have you brought me gold, dear sister,
Or have you bought me free,
Or have you come for to see me hang
All under this gallows tree?"

"I've neither brought you gold, dear brother,
Nor I've neither bought you free,
But I have come for to see you hang,
And hangit you shall be."

"Jimmy Loud, Jimmy Loud, Jimmy Loud," he cries,
"Pray hold your hands for a while,
I think I see my true-love a-coming;
She's been riding so many miles.

"Oh, have you brought me gold, true-love,
And have you bought me free,
Or have you come for to see me hang
All under this gallows tree?"

"Oh, I have brought you gold, true-love,
And I have bought you free,
And I have come for to take you home
From under this gallows tree."

Hangman

COLLECTED IN 1977 BY BURT FEINTUCH FROM THE WALKER FAMILY (BERNICE, VOCAL; SAMMIE AND IVAN, FIDDLES; NELL, GUITAR), BARREN AND METCALFE COUNTIES, KENTUCKY. TRANSCRIPTION BY DREW BEISSWENGER.

Hangman, hangman, hold your rope, hold your rope a little while.
Thought I saw my father a coming, from many, many a mile.

Father, Father, have you gold, have you gold to set me free,
Or have you come to see me hung upon the gallows tree?

Oh, Son, oh, Son, I have no gold, have no gold to set you free.
I have come for to see you hung upon this gallows tree.

Hangman, hangman, hold your rope, hold your rope a little while.
Thought I saw my mother a coming from a many, many a mile.

Mother, Mother, have you gold, have you gold to set me free,
Or have you come for to see me hung upon this gallows tree?

Oh, Son, oh, Son, I have no gold, have no gold to set you free.
I have come for to see you hung upon this gallows tree.

Hangman, hangman, hold your rope, hold your rope a little while.
Thought I saw my sister a coming from a many, many a mile.

Sister, Sister, have you gold, have you gold to set me free,
Have you come to see me hung upon this gallows tree?

Oh, Brother, oh, Brother, I have no gold, have no gold to set you free.
I have come for to see you hung upon this gallows tree.

Hangman, hangman, hold your rope, hold your rope a little while.
Thought I saw my brother a coming from a many, many a mile.

Brother, oh, Brother, have you gold, have you gold to set me free,
Or have you come to see me hung upon this gallows tree?

Oh, Brother, oh, Brother, I have no gold, have no gold to set you free.
I have come for to see you hung upon the gallows tree.

Hangman, hangman, hold your rope, hold your rope a little while,
Thought I saw my sweetheart a coming from a many, many a mile.

Sweetheart, Sweetheart, have you gold, have you gold to set me free,
Have you come to see me hung upon the gallows tree?

Sweetheart, Sweetheart, I have the gold; I have the gold to set you free.
I haven't come to see you hung upon this gallows tree.

This is a version of Child 95, "The Maid Freed From the Gallows," one of the most popular and most frequently studied of the Child ballads. It has been reported from tradition in Virginia, Alabama, Maine, Missouri, North Carolina, Tennessee, South Carolina, West Virginia, Ohio, Vermont, Kentucky, Michigan, Mississippi, Texas, New York, Arkansas, Oklahoma, and Indiana, and is probably even more widely known than that list indicates. It is also popular outside the boundaries of the United States, for it has been collected in the Andros Islands and Jamaica and, of course, is also known in the British Isles and in Europe. Besides Child's title and those used for the two versions given here, the ballad is known as "By a Lover Saved," "Down By the Green Willow," "The Gailant Tree," "The Gallis Pole," "The Gallows Tree," "The Golden Ball," "The Hangman's Song," "Highway Man," "Lord James," "The Miller's Daughter," "The Scarlet Tree," "The Sycamore Tree," "True Love," "Under the Creep-O Mellow Tree," "The Raspel Pole," and "Ropesman, Rop'ry." Among Southern singers the most popular of these numerous titles are "Hangman," "The Hangman's Tree," or "The Gallows Tree."

As found in American tradition, Child 95 consists of seven story types; in the most popular of these a girl is about to be hung on the gallows for an unspecified crime. She asks the hangman to stop the execution because she sees a relative, usually her father, coming. She then asks the relative a series of questions to determine if he has come to set her free. The relative says he has come to see her hang. The same series of questions are asked of several other relatives until her sweetheart comes and sets her free, usually by paying a fee or perhaps by cutting the hangman's rope with a knife. Most of the other story types are variations on this basic narrative. In one the crime of which she was guilty is suggested, in another the prisoner is male, in yet another the maid or man is not rescued, and in still another the fate of the prisoner is not detailed. A sixth story type consists of "The Maid Freed From the Gallows" motif interwoven around several stanzas of blues cliches; the rescue happens in the usual manner. A final type has several stanzas in which the girl speaks to God, and her lover appears and sets her free, as usual.

Francis J. Child, of course, was the first person to trace the history of this ballad, concentrating primarily on its pan-European tradition. Since then extensive studies have been published by Erik Pohl, Iivar Kempinnen, Giovanni Bronzini, Ingeborg Uricia, Dan Ben-Amos, Tristram P. Coffin, and Eleanor Long, among others. Long's book is, by far, the most wide-ranging study of various forms of the ballad even though it overlooks many European variants. Long believes the male sex of the victim is the earliest form and the one most commonly found in tradition, but the sex really depends on regional preferences; the narratives in cante-fable (i.e. "singing tales" or narratives that are partly sung and partly spoken) forms were later additions to an already existing ballad; this ballad was probably introduced into English tradition in the last half of the seventeenth century by gypsies.

The tunes generally associated with this ballad are in common time, usually 2/4 or 4/4 (meaning there are two or four beats in a measure with a quarter note being the kind of note that receives a beat) but occasionally there are versions in compound time, generally 6/8 (meaning six beats to a measure with an eighth note being the type of note that receives a beat). Thus, the melodies given here are typical of the general tradition. The first example of the ballad was collected in April, 1935 by Mercedes Steely from Mrs. Nora Johnson, Ebenezer, North Carolina. For more information about Steely and Johnson see the comments concerning "I Dreamt Last Night of My True Love." Mrs. Johnson, apparently, varied the name at different times, sometimes singing "Jimmy Low" and sometimes "Jimmy Loud." When Steely questioned her about the name, Johnson's husband teased her and tried to get her to decide on one name; she immediately decided upon "Loud." Steely, however, believed that "Low" was the name she originally learned, primarily because a version of the ballad titled "Jimmy Low" has been reported from Virginia.

The second version of Child 95 given here was collected in 1977 by Bert Feintuch from Bernice Walker, Barren County, Kentucky. Walker is a member of a family well known locally for their music, much of which has been recorded for the Western Kentucky University Folklore Archive starting as far back as the late 1950s. Currently three generations of her family are active musicians. Most of the ballads she knows, such as this one, come from her mother.

COLLECTED BY GEORGE FOSS FROM ROBERT SHIFLETT, BROWN'S COVE, VIRGINIA,
1961. TRANSCRIPTION BY GEORGE FOSS.

An old knight rode one summer's day,
Down by the greenwood side;
And there he spied a fair young maid,
And all alone she cried.

As he drew nearer unto her,
To learn what it could mean,
All her lamentation was
For John of Hazelgreen.

"You're welcome home, my fair young one,
You're welcome home with me,
And you may wed my oldest son,
A bold young man is he."

"I would not wed your oldest son,
If he were lord or king,
For I never intend to be the bride of none,
Save John of Hazelgreen."

"Oh, he is tall, his shoulders broad,
He's the fairest of the king,
His hair hangs down in links of gold,
My John of Hazelgreen."

He took her up before him then,
And they rode near the town,
Bold John of Hazelgreen sprang out,
To lift his lady down.

Three times he kissed her ruby lips,
Three times he kissed her chin,
He took her by her fair white hand,
To lead his lady in.

The tears were dry, the sorrow gone,
But her surprise was seen,
To learn the old knight's eldest son
Was John of Hazelgreen.

"If I should ever thee forsake,
May heaven forsake me,
And cast me in the brimstone lake
Forever and eternity."

This ballad, which Child listed as 293 under the title given here, is rare in American tradition. It has been reported from Maine, Virginia, Vermont, Florida, Oklahoma, and Newfoundland but most versions seem to be from "memory culture" rather than from a vital tradition. There is very little variation in titles, usually replacing John for Jack or Jock, although there is a "Willie of Hazelgreen" as well as a "Johnny From Hazelgreen." This small degree of variation is possibly an indication of the ballad's tenuous traditional life. Also possibly attesting to its rarity is the fact that there are only two story types found in American tradition. Basically the narrative consists of a man discovering a young girl crying. He offers her his oldest son in marriage; she refuses saying she loves John of Hazelgreen. The girl then rides to a nearby town where she meets John, who kisses her and promises fidelity. The second type, represented by the present version, has the girl ride home with the man. On the way she is met by John, who turns out to be the son.

Much of the literature dealing with this ballad concerns its relationship with Sir Walter Scott's "Jock of Hazeldean" (1816). It is certain that the Scott ballad is partially derived from the traditional ballad, the debate being over the extent of the borrowing. Child believed Scott took only one stanza from popular balladry; Maurice W. Kelley argued, however, that Scott borrowed a great deal of the song from the traditional ballad. In the most recent discussion of the matter Charles G. Zug III maintains that Scott wrote the entire song but modeled it closer to traditional style than was the case with his earlier compositions. At this point in time definitive conclusions are probably impossible, any determinations having to depend to some degree upon faith and assumption.

The present text was collected by George Foss, July 15, 1961, from Robert Shiflett, Brown's Cove, Virginia. Shiflett learned most of his songs from his family and other members of his community. For more information about him see the notes for "Texas Rangers."

Lord Lovel

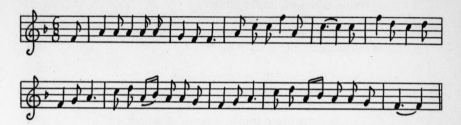

COLLECTED BY MARION TAYLOR PAGE FROM NANCY McCUDDY STEVENSON, ST. BETHLEHEM, TENNESSEE. EXACT DATE OF COLLECTION NOT GIVEN BUT WAS SOMETIME BETWEEN 1953–1955. TRANSCRIPTION BY MARION TAYLOR PAGE.

Lord Lovel stood at the castle gate,
　　Combing his milk white steed,
When out came Lady Nancy Belle,
　　Bidding her lover good speed, speed, speed,
Bidding her lover good speed.

"Where are you going, Lord Lovel?" she said.
　　"Where are you going?" said she.
"I'm going away, my Nancy Belle,
　　Strange countries for to see, see, see,
Strange countries for to see."

"When will you be back, Lord Lovel?" said she.
　　"When will you be back?" said she.
"In a year or two or three at most,
　　I'll return to my Lady Nancee, cee, cee,
I'll return to my Lady Nancee."

He rode and rode his milk white steed,
　　Strange countries for to see,
'Till languishing thoughts came over his mind
　　Concerning his Lady Nancee, cee, cee,
Concerning his Lady Nancee.

He hadn't been gone but a year and a day
　　When he returned to London town,
And there he heard the church bells ring,
　　And the people all mourning around, 'round, 'round,
And the people all mourning around.

"What is the matter?" Lord Lovel, he said.
   "What is the matter?" said he.
"A great Lord's lady has died today,
   And some called her Lady Nancee, cee, cee,
And some called her Lady Nancee."

He ordered the grave to be opened wide,
   And the shroud to be laid aside.
And there he kissed her clay cold lips
   'Till the tears come trickling down, down, down,
'Till the tears came trickling down.

Lady Nancy she died as you might say today.
   Lord Lovel he died tomorrow.
Lady Nancy she died of pure pure love.
   Lord Lovel he died of sorrow, sorrow, sorrow.
Lord Lovel he died of sorrow.

Lady Nancy was buried in St. Patrick's church.
   Lord Lovel was buried in the choir.
And out of her bosom there grew a red rose,
   And out of Lord Lovel's a briar, briar, briar,
And out of Lord Lovel's a briar.

They grew and they grew to the church steeple's top,
   Until they could grow no higher.
They twined themselves in a true lovers' knot
   For all true lovers to admire, 'mire, 'mire,
For all true lovers to admire.

Listed under the present title as number 75 in Child's collection, this ballad has proven to be very popular in American tradition. To date it has been reported from Texas, Oklahoma, Utah, Alabama, New York, Maine, Missouri, North Carolina, South Carolina, Indiana, Tennessee, West Virginia, Virginia, Ohio, Vermont, Michigan, Mississippi, Kentucky, Florida, Pennsylvania, Nebraska, and Maryland. Yet, despite its great popularity, the ballad shows little variation either in story, tune, or titles. Most of the titles are some variation of "Lord Lovel" or "Lady Nancy," such as "Nancy Bell and Lord Lover." There are only two story types in American tradition and they are very similar. One is essentially that given in the present text. The second type is the same except that Lovel returns after only two or three miles of travel when a ring on his finger "busts off" and his nose begins to bleed. Lady Nancy's funeral bells are being sounded before he is halfway back.

Lack of great variation is usually interpreted to mean that a song is not far from print or mass media sources. This seems to be true of "Lord Lovel" for, although the earliest reports of the ballad are from eighteenth century England, most American versions seem to be directly or indirectly derived from a London broadside of 1846. This version appeared in a number of pre-Civil War songbooks and broadsides. Parodists of the Civil War era frequently utilized the song, indicating that it was a favorite ballad of the time; a parody taunting Abraham Lincoln on his military reverses was once quite popular in the South. As recently as the turn of the century the ballad was still being parodied, as is attested by Carolyn Wells's *A Parody Anthology* (New York: Charles Scribner's Sons, 1904), p. 326.

The present version was collected sometime between 1953–1955 (exact date is not given) by Marion Taylor Page from Nancy McCuddy Stevenson, St. Bethlehem, Tennessee. Mrs. Stevenson learned her songs around 1900 from both her mother and her father, although it is not stated which parent was the source of "Lord Lovel."

Molly Van

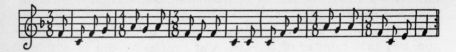

COLLECTED JUNE 1, 1962 BY GEORGE FOSS FROM DAN TATE, FANCY GAP, VIRGINIA.
TRANSCRIPTION BY DAN BRACKIN.

Come all you young men who handle a gun,
Beware of your shooting just after set sun.
Jimmy Randall went hunting it was all in the dark,
He shot at his sweetheart and he missed not his mark.

Stooped under a beech tree a shower to shun,
With her apron pinned around he shot her for a swan.
Young Jimmy went home with his gun in his hand,
Saying, "Father, dear father, I've killed Molly Van.

"I've killed this fair maiden, I've taken her life,
And I always intended to have made her my wife."
On the day of Jimmy's trial Molly's ghost did appear
Saying, "Jimmy Randall, Jimmy Randall goes clear."

Come all you young maidens and stand you in a row,
Molly Van is in the middle as a mountain of snow.

Some collectors have found this ballad especially appealing and have waxed rhapsodic about it. Cecil Sharp thought it "a strange admixture of fancy with matter of fact," opining that it might be a survival from either the Celtic or Norse past. Alas for his theory, it is a British broadside that first appeared in print in Robert Jamieson's *Popular Ballads and Songs* (1806) under the title "Lord Kenneth and Fair Ellinour." Jamieson had it from Professor Robert Scott of King's College, Aberdeen, who had taken it down from the recitation of one of his maids. Apparently, the ballad was known in Scotland as "Peggy Baun" and it has come to be known traditionally in America under several different titles including "Molly Vaughn," "Polly Van," "Molly Banding," "Molly Vaunders," "Polly Bon," and "Polly Bond." Generally, though, it is known in the United States as "Molly Bawn" or "Shooting of His Dear." There is little variation on the basic story type although some versions lack the appearance of Molly's ghost to free her lover from the murder charge. The loss of this detail in many versions is probably part of the general American tendency to lose supernatural elements. Even so, most such texts have been regarded as incomplete by their singers, indicating either that some words were forgotten or that they never knew the complete ballad. Most texts have the man named Jimmy or Jimmy Randall, although in several versions he is unnamed and referred to as "her true love" or in some similar way.

The present text was collected June 1, 1962 by George Foss from Dan Tate, Fancy Gap, Virginia. Tate was born in 1900 in Carroll County, Virginia and still lives there. He is known not only for his singing but his banjo playing, a fact that refutes Cecil Sharp's contention that banjo playing and ballad singing were not compatible. Tate's large repertoire of old songs and tunes has made him a favorite informant for a number of folksong and ballad collectors. He performs "Molly Van" in his usual smooth, controlled style, but *a cappella* rather than to banjo accompaniment that he uses for most songs. Tate's source for this ballad is not given.

Seated One Day in a Beautiful Cafe

COLLECTED JANUARY 21, 1966 BY SUE FRAZIER FROM RALPH E. FRAZIER, MORRISON CITY, TENNESSEE. TRANSCRIPTION BY ANNETTE WOLFORD.

I was seated one day in a beautiful cafe
   on a window that looked to the street;
And a face caught my eye in a crowd that passed by,
   and I hastently spring to my feet.
'Twas my sister's sad face I had left home to trace;
   through her pride she had left us one day,
And it brought back to me just as plain as could be
   my mother as I heard her say:

CHORUS:
"If you should see your sister, do not reproach her, Dwayne;
Just tell her that we miss her and love her just the same;
Tell her these words that you brought her sadness love refrain;
Tell her that she is my daughter; whisper your mother's name."

There was tears on her face as she passed by this place,
    and I hastenly spring to her side,
And as we walked along I says, "Nell, we were wrong
    and we're sorry we wounded your pride.
Your sweetheart is true, and he's waiting for you;
    we willingly now that you wed;
And if you will come back, you can marry your Jack
    and please your dear mother that's dead."

CHORUS: (same as before)

When it originally appeared this song was popularized by Lottie Gilson (1869–1912), one of the most successful singers of the 1890s. Gilson was called "America's greatest serio-comic" but was more commonly billed as "The Little Magnet." The latter sobriquet referred to Gilson's drawing power; she generally had standing-room only crowds wherever she appeared even though they frequently had to pay the then-exorbitant sum of fifty cents a head. Originally Gilson was known for tear-jerkers like "The Old Turnkey," "The Old Sexton," and "The Little Lost Child," but later she turned to numbers like "She's Such a Nice Girl, Too" and "Sunshine of Paradise Alley," songs then considered slightly risque. Besides the various tunes she introduced, which included "The Sidewalks of New York," Gilson is today remembered for two reasons. She was the first singer to accept money to "plug" a song, and she introduced the idea of having a stooge planted in the balcony to sing and talk back to her. The latter stunt was done to death by other performers; eventually a song, "The Singer in the Gallery," was written about the phenomenon and it became a popular number on the vaudeville circuit.

One of Gilson's hits of 1896 was "Whisper Your Mother's Name," the original title of the ballad given here. Both it and Gilson's other 1896 success, "You're Not the Only Pebble on the Beach," were written by two young Yale graduates, Harry B. Berdan and Frederick J. Redcliffe who used the pseudonyms of Harry Braisted and Stanley Carter. Besides these two songs, Berdan and Redcliffe's biggest numbers were "She Was Bred in Old Kentucky" (now remembered largely because it inspired the parody "She was bred in Old Kentucky, She was cake in New Orleans, She was clam chowder in New England, But in Boston she was beans") and "The Girl I Loved in Sunny Tennessee" (both 1898). The latter song remains popular today with traditional country and bluegrass performers. Berdan and Redcliffe had no further successes, even of a minor nature, but "She Was Bred in Old Kentucky" turned up in 1909 as the tune of the chorus to A. Baldwin Sloane's satirical "Heaven Will Protect the Working Girl."

"Seated One Day in a Beautiful Cafe" was collected January 21, 1966 by Sue Frazier from the singing of Ralph E. Frazier. Unfortunately, no further information is available about either the collector or singer. Enough of the wording is changed to indicate that Frazier had this ballad from oral tradition rather than from a copy of the original sheet music. Such words as "hastently" and the phrase "we willingly now that you wed" are different from the original lyrics and are probably misunderstandings of words or phrases. Whatever the case, they are the types of changes that usually occur first when a ballad enters oral tradition. The male figure's name of Dwayne is somewhat unusual for a ballad; in fact, this may be the only traditional ballad where the major male character has this name.

Ballads of Unfaithful Lovers

Barb'ry Allen

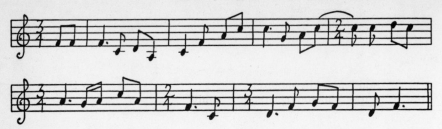

COLLECTED BY BYRON ARNOLD FROM CALLIE CRAVEN, GADSDEN, ALABAMA, NOVEMBER 26, 1946. TRANSCRIPTION BY BYRON ARNOLD.

Lonely lonely was a town
Where three fair maids were dwelling;
There was but one that I called my own
And that was Barb'ry Allen.

He sent his servant to the town
Where these fair maids were dwelling,
"My master's sick and he's very sick
And for your sake he's dyin'."

Slowly, slowly she rose up
And to his bed side going
She drew the curtain to one side
And said, "Young man, you're a-dyin'."

He turned his pale face to the wall
His back towards his darling,
"Adieu, adieu to the friends around
Be kind to Barb'ry Allen."

As she was walking through the field
She heard a death bell tolling;
She looked to the east and she looked to the west
And saw the corpse a-coming.

"Lay down, lay down the corpse," she said,
"That I may kiss upon him."
The more she kissed and the more she grieved,
And bursted out a-cryin'.

"Oh mother, oh mother, make my bed,
Go make it long and narrow;
Sweet William died for me today
I'll die for him tomorrow."

Sweet William died on Saturday night
And Barb'ry died on Sunday;
The old lady died for the love of both
And was buried Easter Monday.

Sweet William's buried in one church yard
And Barb'ry in another;
A rose bud sprang from one church yard
And a brier from the other.

They grew and they grew until they grew so tall
They could not grow any higher;
They linked and tied in a true love's knot
That all true lovers might admire.

This is without question the most popular of the Child ballads in America and one of the most popular of all ballads in the oral tradition. It is well-known not only to folklorists but to popular singers and writers as well, as is attested by a recording by Maxine Sullivan and a lengthy discussion in Peter Taylor's *The Old Forest and Other Stories* (1985). Listed as number 84 it appears in Child's collection as "Bonny Barbara Allen." It is also known traditionally as "Barbara Allen's Cruelty," "Barbarous Ellen," "Edelin," "Little Johnnie Green," "Sir John Graham," "Mary Alling," and "Barbry Alone." Thirteen different story types have been identified in America, most of them featuring the summons to the death-bed, Barbara's indifferent compliance with it, and the intertwining of the symbolic plants from the graves. To date more than 600 texts of "Barbara Allen" have been recorded in the United States.

The exact age of "Barbara Allen" is unknown but it was around in the seventeenth century. Samuel Pepys, writing in his diary for January 2, 1666, comments that he heard a Mrs. Knipp, an actress, singing "her little Scotch song of Barbry Allen." Despite Pepys' statement that it is a Scottish song the earliest known Scottish text is in Allan Ramsay's *Tea Table Miscellany* (1740). Mrs. Knipp's background is not known although, possibly, she was from Scotland which would explain Pepys' attribution. The earliest known text, however, is an English broadside published in Pepys' lifetime and included in Thomas Percy's *Reliques of Ancient English Poetry* (1765). "Barbara Allen"'s appearance on these and several other broadsides and its frequent inclusion in songbooks has undoubtedly aided its popularity. The earliest known American broadside is dated 1840 but there are several American songbook printings predating 1840, the earliest possibly being in the *American Songster* (c. 1829).

Published versions, however, should not be given too much credit for perpetuating and propagating the ballad. After all, the printers were interested in making money and were not just printing any songs but rather those that already had a certain degree of popular favor. Yet, "Barbara Allen" 's great popularity is not easy to explain, given its seemingly undistinguished, unexciting content, its fatalistic story of willing submission to ill fortune, and its lack of suspense, surprise, or violence. The male figure is hardly heroic, he is rather a passive, somewhat spineless character who readily resigns to accepting his fate. There is not even the soap opera element of a love triangle and the "heroine" is also passive and generally somewhat cruel. These characters and the ballad in which they figure are seemingly not the stuff of which truly memorable songs are made. Yet, "Barbara Allen" is not only remembered but, if there were a Hit Parade of traditional ballads would most likely be in the number one position. So, how can its great popularity be explained?

There are a number of evident features that can be cited which help elucidate the matter of "Barbara Allen" 's popularity. One is the fact that it is an easy song to remember, in fact, it is almost impossible to get the story twisted. There are only two characters who are distinguished by word and deed in a critical situation. The "heroine's" name is euphonious and serves, in most versions, as a memory aid for the stanzaic rhymes simultaneously pointing out the successive phases of the narrative: dwelling, swelling, telling, knelling. Moreover, the double rhyme is its own mnemonic device. Furthermore, the tunes for all versions of "Barbara Allen" are very memorable, with simple and familiar rhythms. There is also a certain romantic appeal to a story that tells of a love so intense and all-consuming that it can cause one's death. Indeed, the idea of love as a destructive force has a long history in Western civilization. There may, of course, be other factors that help explain the ballad's popularity but these seem to be the most important.

The girl's name rarely varies but her lover is known by several first names including William, Willie, James, Jemmy, Jimmy, and John. Frequently his last name is not given but those texts that do provide it have him named Grove, Groves, Green, Grame, Graham, Hilliard, Ryley, and Rosie. The rose-briar motif, common in American texts, does not appear in the three texts given by Child. In those traditional texts lacking that motif the ballad usually concludes with either "a warning to all virgins" or with a "turtle dove and sparrow" stanza. The ballad's action usually takes place in May or autumn and is set in "Scarlet town." Some authorities believe that originally it was set in "Reading town," hence the Scarlet town setting is a pun. Occasionally, the story occurs in some other locality, such as Reading, Dallas, or New York.

The main narrative variations involve the actions of Barbara and her lover regarding the accusation, defense, and parting. Many of the common features found in American texts, such as the lover's curse on Barbara, Barbara's curse of the lover, and the lover's acknowledgment of Barbara's charges, are not present in Child's texts and are thought to have originated with the broadside and songbook texts. An interesting feature of several versions is the ballad's shift from first to third person in the course of the narrative.

The present text was collected November 26, 1946, by Byron Arnold from Callie Craven, Gadsden, Alabama. Craven (1871–1946) was the first singer Arnold recorded material from while putting together the items for his *Folksongs of Alabama* (1950).* She was very glad that Arnold wished to include her songs in a book and she willingly recorded for him on several occasions although, owing to frail health, she could only sing for a short time without tiring. Craven learned most of her songs from her mother, a native of Charleston, South Carolina. The family was destitute and when Callie was eighteen a Mr. B.W. Duke "adopted" them, providing a house on his farm. In return, Craven helped raise Duke's six children, one of which recalled that she frequently sang ballads and folksongs while rocking them to sleep. She also loved to sing for company or at various local entertainments. She was illiterate so her songs represent a strictly oral tradition.

*A new edition of *Folksongs of Alabama* is being prepared by Dr. Robert Halli and will be published by the University of Alabama Press.

The Broken-hearted Boy

COLLECTED BY THEODORE GARRISON FROM MRS. BERTHA TUEL, MARSHALL,
ARKANSAS, APRIL, 1941. TRANSCRIPTION BY THEODORE GARRISON.

There was a wealthy farmer
    In Texas near Austin did dwell.
He had a beautiful daughter,
    The one I love so well;
She was so young and beautiful,
    Brown eyes and curly hair,
There is no other in Texas
    With her I can compare.

I went to see this pretty fair maiden;
    I asked her if she would be mine.
She hung her head in deep study,
    Like wishing to decline.
Says I, "The question is left with you;
    Go answer if you can.
But, Love, if I don't suit you,
    Go choose you another man."

She raised her head while smiling,
    Saying, "Love, I'm bound to say 'yes'.
You seem so honest and truthful,
    And you'll prove so, I guess.
But if you'll promise to marry me,
    I'll marry no other man;
So here is my heart, come and take it."
    She gave me her right hand.

I asked her if she'd wait awhile
    Till I could go away,
Till I could go and raise a stake;
    I would return some day.
She hung her head in deep sorrow
    And looked most scornfully;
We kissed, shook hands, and parted,
    I left her to mourn for me.

So now, my kind friends, I must leave you;
　　I am inclined to go.
And sure and well he mounted
　　And drilled to Old Mexico.
It's when I get there, if not suited,
　　I'll drill to some foreign land;
But I never can forget the farmer's girl
　　That gave me her right hand.

I stayed six months in Old Mexico,
　　And when I changed my mind.
I drilled up into old Kansas,
　　Where ladies treated me fine.
It was there I found fine country,
　　Fine houses, and fine land;
But I never can forget the farmer's girl
　　That gave me her right hand.

I went to Kansas City
　　One evening bright and fair.
I stopped off into a post office;
　　The mail was arriving there.
I received a letter from Texas
　　Which I was glad to see;
I thought it was from the farmer's girl
　　That said she would marry me.

The post office being crowded,
　　I stepped off to one side
To read this letter from Texas,
　　Which was written both long and wide;
And on it I found my mother's name,
　　And this is what she said,
"The farmer's girl you love so well,
　　I'm sorry to say, she is dead."

This filled my heart with deep sorrow;
　　I knew not what to do.
While folding up this letter,
　　I knew those words were true.
I'm going back to old Texas
　　To live a bachelor's life,
For the farmer's girl I love so well
　　She never can be my wife.

While on my way to old Texas,
    I stopped in El Paso town;
Got in with a bunch of gay cowboys
    To ramble the city around.
To drive away all sorrow
    I taken a glass of wine;
But the love I had for the farmer's girl,
    She never would leave my mind.

This song originated as a British broadside which is commonly known as "The Girl I Left Behind" but also as "My Parents Treated Me Tenderly," "The Maid I Left Behind," and "The Girl I Left On New River," among others. There are two ballads known as "The Girl I Left Behind" (not to be confused with "The Girl I Left Behind Me"), both of British broadside origin and telling similar stories. In one the narrator promises to be faithful to his sweetheart before he leaves her to travel to a distant city where he finds another girl. After marrying his new lover he is haunted by thoughts of his parents and his girl, who have died of broken hearts. In the other ballad, which is more common in America, it is the girl left behind who is unfaithful and marries another. Sometimes the narrator refuses the hand of his new acquaintance before learning of his girl's unfaithfulness. Usually he is so disheartened by the news that he resolves to spend the rest of his life in gambling or drinking or both but, in a Scottish text titled "All Frolicking I'll Give Over," the narrator marries after learning that his former sweetheart is already wed. In the present text no real unfaithfulness is detailed, although the protagonist notes "ladies treated me fine," but his sweetheart presumably died from a broken heart. Thus, it has elements of both ballads but seems closest to the second.

Widely known in America, "The Girl I Left Behind" has been reported from most of the Southern states as well as from Minnesota, Missouri, and Wisconsin. N. Howard "Jack" Thorp, an early collector of cowboy songs, claimed a text titled "The Rambling Cowboy" that he printed in the revised version of *Songs of the Cowboys* (1921) was written by a K. Tolliver. In light of what is known about the song's history this claim should not be taken too seriously. If Tolliver had any hand in the song's creation it was merely to rework some already existing lyrics. In *Cowboy Songs* (1938), John Lomax gives an unusually long text titled "Lackey Bill" which has several stanzas not found elsewhere. Since Lomax is notorious for "improving" his texts it seems likely that this is a composite effort, not a version that anyone ever sang.

Most versions of the ballad do not provide any kind of moralizing ending, concluding usually with the narrator's decision to spend the remainder of his life in dissipation. An exception to this general rule is found in a text collected by Chauncey and Ethel Moore in Bristow, Oklahoma. Their version concludes with a warning:

> Come, all you reckless and rambling boys
> Who have listened to my song,
> If it's done no good, sir,
> I'm sure it's done no wrong.
> But when you court a pretty girl,
> Just marry her when you can;
> For if you ever cross those plains,
> She'll marry another man.

The version given here was collected by Theodore Garrison from Mrs. Bertha Tuel, Marshall, Arkansas, in April, 1941. At the time of collection Mrs. Tuel was about thirty-seven years old and a farm wife. Her father was well known locally for his fiddle playing, and she used to accompany him on a reed organ. Her father was her source for this ballad and most of the other songs she knew.

The Fatal Wedding

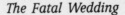

COLLECTED BY BYRON ARNOLD FROM GERTRUDE LADNIER CROOKS, POINT CLEAR,
ALABAMA, JULY 7, 1947. TRANSCRIPTION BY BYON AROLD.

The wedding bells were ringing on a moonlit winter's night
The church was decorated, all within was gay and bright.
A woman with a baby came and saw the lights aglow,
She thought of how those same bells chimed for her three years ago.
I'd like to be admitted, sir, she told the sexton old
Just for the sake of baby to protect him from the cold.
He told her that the wedding was for the rich and grand,
And with the eager watching crowd, outside she'd have to stand.

While the wedding bells were ringing,
While the bride and groom were there,
Marching up the aisle together,
While the organ pealed an air;
And tales of fond affection,
Vowing never more to part,
Just another fatal wedding,
Just another broken heart.

She asked the sexton once again to let her pass inside.
"For baby's sake you may step in," the gray-haired man replied;
"If any one knows reason why this couple should not wed,
Speak now, or forever hold your peace," the preacher soon said!
"I must object," the woman cried, with voice so meek and mild,
"The bridegroom is my husband, sir, and this our little child."
"What proof have you?" the preacher said. "My infant," she replied.
She raised her babe, then knelt to pray, the little one had died.

The parents of the bride then took the outcast by the arm.
"We'll care for you through life," they said, "you've saved our child from
    harm."
The outcast wife, the bride and parents, quickly drove away,
The husband died by his own hand, before the break of day!
No wedding feast was spread that night, two graves were made next day,
One for the little baby, and in one the father lay.
The story has been often told, by firesides warm and bright,
Of bride and groom, of outcast, and that fatal wedding night.

While this story may seem preposterous to some, it has considerable appeal to folksingers. It was one of the biggest hits of Negro
songwriter Gussie L. Davis (1863–1899), who is one of the most interesting figures in American popular music of the late nineteenth century.
A totally self-taught musician, he frequently supplied melodies far better
than the lyrics he had to work with. Reportedly he picked up some of the
elements of composition while working as a janitor at the Cincinnati
Conservatory of Music. Whatever the situation, he demonstrated an
almost uncanny ability to produce songs that sounded "white" and,
apparently, possessed unending interest to folksingers. His first
successes came in the 1880s with "We Sat Beneath the Maple on the Hill"
(1885) and "The Lighthouse by the Sea" (1886). In the 1890s he produced
"If I Only Could Blot Out the Past" (1893), "Picture 84" (1894), "Down in
Poverty Row" (1895), and "In the Baggage Coach Ahead" (1896). Several
of these songs are still found in traditional repertoires.

William H. Windom, a popular actor of the day, supplied the words
to "The Fatal Wedding," dedicating this example of infidelity, sudden
death, and artificial melodrama to the *Utica* (New York) *Tribune.* Davis's
melody was much more elaborate than the words, combining a touch of
the Mendelssohn Wedding March with chime effects and melody
decorations in the chorus. Most of these features are missing from traditional performances of the piece; the solemn sincerity of the lyrics
usually dominate. The ballad appeared on several commercial recordings, of which Bradley Kincaid's was probably the most commercially
successful.

The present text was collected July 7, 1947 by Byron Arnold from the singing of Gertrude Ladnier Crooks, Point Clear, Alabama. Crooks was accompanied by the fiddle playing of Sidney Ladnier who is probably her brother. Crooks tried once before to sing this song but forgot the words in the middle of the piece and had to start over. Unfortunately, Arnold tells nothing more about either the informant or the recording situation. Also unfortunate is his transcription of the melody, for it is clearly incomplete but, because it is the way Arnold transcribed it, it is given here.

I'll Hang My Harp on a Willow Tree

COLLECTED BY ARTHUR PALMER HUDSON FROM MRS. H. M. STRINGER, HAMBURG, MISSISSIPPI.

I'll hang my harp on a willow tree
And off to the wars again;
My peaceful home hath no charm for me
The battlefield no pain.
The lady I love will soon be a bride
With a diadem on her brow.
Why did she flatter my boyish pride?
She's going to leave me now.

She took me away from my warlike accord
And gave me a silken suit,
I thought no more of my master's sword
As I played on my master's lute.
She seemed to think me a boy above
Her pages of low degree;
Oh! Why did she flatter my boyish pride?
She's going to leave me now.

One golden tress of her hair I'll twine
In my helmet an able plume
And then on the field of the Palestine
I'll seek an early doom;
And if by the Saracens' hand fall
'Mid the noble and the brave;
A tear from my gay deceiver is all
I ask for a warrior's grave.

I'll Hang My Harp on a Willow Tree

AS GIVEN IN *HEART SONGS*.

I'll hang my harp on a willow tree,
I'll off to the wars again,
My peaceful home has no charms for me,
The battlefield no pain;
The lady I love will soon be a bride,
With a diadem on her brow.
Oh! why did she flatter my boyish pride,
She's going to leave me now.

She took me away from my warlike lord,
And gave me a silken suit,
I tho't no more of my master's sword,
But play'd my master's lute;
She seem'd to think me a boy above
Her pages of low degree,
Oh! had I but lov'd with a boyish love,
It would have been better for me.

Then I'll hide in my breast ev'ry selfish care,
I'll flush my pale cheek with wine;
When smiles awake the bridal pair,
I'll hasten to give them mine.
I'll laugh and I'll sing tho' my heart may bleed,
And I'll walk in the festive train,
And if I survive it I'll mount my steed,
And off to the wars again.

But one golden tress of her hair I'll twine,
In my helmet's sable plume,
And then on the field of Palestine
I'll seek an early doom;
And if by the Saracen's hand I fall,
'Mid the noble and the brave,
A tear from my Lady love is all
I ask for the warrior's grave.

Some people have claimed that this song is of ancient English origin (one of them being folksinger Almeda Riddle [1898–1986]) but in some nineteenth-century songbooks it is attributed to a W. Guernsey. This was Wellington Guernsey who is listed as the lyricist-composer on a sheet music edition published in Louisville, Kentucky in 1848 or 1849 by W.C. Peters & Co. At least two possibilities exist concerning Guernsey's connection with the song. First, it is possible that he was merely an arranger and had nothing to do with the creation of the ballad. The fact that he is given total credit on the sheet music does not preclude this possibility. A second probability is that Guernsey wrote the lyrics and set them to an older tune; this would explain the frequent references to the song as an ancient English number. However, approximately two years before the Guernsey edition appeared, a sheet music edition, arranged for voice and guitar, was published in Philadelphia. This edition of c. 1846 was arranged by Leopold Meignen and made no mention of Guernsey. It apparently was fairly widely known by the 1850s, for a parody titled "I'll Hang My Nose On a Forked Stick" appeared at the head of a chapter in David Rattlehead's *The Life and Adventures of an Arkansaw Doctor* (1852).

The first version given here was collected in the late 1920s by Arthur Palmer Hudson from Mrs. H.M. Stringer of Hamburg, Mississippi. Hudson (1892–1978) was a longtime teacher at the University of Mississippi and at the University of North Carolina who is primarily remembered in folklore for his *Folksongs of Mississippi* (1936). He provided no further information about Mrs. Stringer except her name and place of residence. It is unclear whether she sang the song or merely wrote down the words, in any case no melody is provided. The tune given here is taken from *Heart Songs,* a 1909 volume resulting from a search initiated by *National Magazine* in 1905 to find the favorite songs of the American people. It is possible this is the melody, or very similar to it, known by Mrs. Stringer. Her lyrics show strong similarity to those found in *Heart Songs* but sufficient differences to indicate that her direct source was not this published form. Such disagreements as "accord" rather than "warlike lord" do not sound entirely logical but are certainly evidence that Stringer's source was likely an oral one.

Jack and Joe

COLLECTED BY GEORGE FOSS FROM OBEY JOHNSON, CROSSNORE, NORTH CAROLINA, 1962. TRANSCRIPTION BY GEORGE FOSS.

Three years ago both Jack and Joe
Set sail across the foam.
Each vowed a fortune they would earn
Before returning home.
In one short year Jack gained his wealth
And set for home that day,
And as the boys shook hands to part,
Poor Joe could only say:

CHORUS:
"Give my love to Nellie, Jack,
And tell her I am well.
Sweetest girl in all this world,
I'm sure you'll say 'tis she.
Treat her kindly, Jack old pal
And tell her I am well;
And don't forget the parting words—
Jack, give my love to Nell."

Three years had passed when Joe at last
Gained wealth enough for life.
He started home across the foam
To make sweet Nell his wife.
But on his way he heard them say
That Jack and Nell had wed;
And deeply he regretted then
That he had ever said:

116

CHORUS:
"Give my love to Nellie, Jack,
And kiss her once for me.
Sweetest girl in all this world,
I'm sure you'll say 'tis she.
Treat her kindly, Jack old pal
And tell her I am well;
And don't forget these parting words—
Jack, give my love to Nell."

Upon the street they chanced to meet
Joe said, "You selfish elf;
The very next girl I learn to love
I'll kiss her for myself.
But all is fair in love, they say,
And since you're truly wed,
And don't forget the parting words,
Jack, give my love to Nell."

CHORUS:
"Give my love to Nellie, Jack,
And kiss her once for me.
Sweetest girl in all this world,
I'm sure you'll say 'tis she.
Treat her kindly, Jack old pal
And tell her I am well;
And don't forget these parting words—
Jack, give my love to Nell."

This ballad was written in 1894 by William B. Gray, a vaudevillian who got his start in show business as a member of the Glenroy Brothers, exhibition boxers. As a songwriter Gray (Glenroy) achieved several successes in the 1890s, among them "The Volunteer Organist" (1893), the present song, "Old Jim's Christmas Hymn" (1896), and "She's More to Be Pitied Than Censured" (1898). He even tried his hand at making a song of the poem "The Picture on the Floor" (generally known as "The Face on the Barroom Floor") but it wasn't very successful. Gray (Glenroy) was also active as a singer, usually teaming as part of a duet with Henry Lamb. The singing partners also were involved in the music publishing business, Glenroy using his pseudonym Gray and Lamb using that of George Spaulding. Although Gray–Lamb's publishing company had a number of successful publications it is remembered today primarily as one of George M. Cohan's first employers.

Gray's song has been reported from traditional singers in Kentucky, Tennessee, Missouri, Illinois, Florida, Utah, and North Carolina. It is likely, though, that the ballad would be reported even more often except that many collectors are prejudiced against material that originated in Tin Pan Alley and have simply ignored it. Most texts reported to date show only minor variations and changes from version to version, suggesting that it is still largely dependent on mass media sources such as commercial records.

The version given here was collected September 2, 1962 by George Foss from Obey Johnson of Crossnore, North Carolina. Unfortunately, no information is available concerning this informant.

Little Massie Grove

COLLECTED OCTOBER 25, 1976 BY KIP LORNELL FROM RUBY BOWMAN PLEMMONS, MEADOWS OF DAN, VIRGINIA. TRANSCRIPTION BY W. K. McNEIL.

My high, my high, my high holiday
And the very first day in the year.
Little Massie Grove to the church did go,
The gospel for to hear, hear,
The gospel for to hear.

The first one in was a fair lady,
And the next one was a girl,
And the next one was Lord Darnold's wife,
And the fairest of them all, all,
And the fairest of them all.

Little Massie Grove was standing by
To him she cast an eye,
Saying, "You must go home with me today
All night in my arms to lie, lie,
All night in my arms to lie."

"Oh no, Oh no," said little Massie Grove,
"I daresn't for my life,
For I can tell by the ring that you wear on your hand,
That you are Lord Darnold's wife."

"Why should we hold such vows sacred,
When he's so far away,
He's gone on top of the King's mountain,
Prince Henry for to see, see
Prince Henry for to see."

So they went home, huggin' and a-kissin',
And then they fell asleep,
But when they awoke on the next day's morn,
Lord Darnold stood at their feet, feet
Lord Darnold stood at their feet.

Saying, "How do you like my new coverlet,
And how do you like my sheets?
How do you like my fair young wife
Who lies in your arms and sleeps, sleeps
Who lies in your arms and sleeps?"

"Pretty well do I like your new coverlet,
Pretty well do I like your sheet,
But much better do I like your fair young wife,
Who lies in my arms and sleeps, sleeps
Who lies in my arms and sleeps."

"Rise up, rise up little Massie Grove,
Put on your clothes just as quick as you can,
It shall never be said in this wide world,
That I slayed a naked man, man
That I slayed a naked man."

"Oh no, Oh, no," said the little Massie Grove,
"I daresn't for my life,
For around your waist you have two swords
And me not as much as a knife, knife
And me not as much as a knife."

"If around my waist I have two swords,
And you not as much as a knife,
Then you may take the best of them,
And then I'll take your life, life
And then I'll take your life.

"And you may strike the first blow,
Now strike it like a man,
And I will strike the next blow,
And I'll kill you if I can, can
And I'll kill you if I can."

So little Massie Grove struck the first blow,
It wounded deep and sore,
But Lord Darnold struck the next blow,
Little Massie couldn't fight no more, more
Little Massie couldn't fight no more.

Then he took his lady by the hand,
And he set her on his knee,
Saying, "Which one do you love the best,
Little Massie Grove or me, me
Little Massie Grove or me?"

"Pretty well do I like your deep blue eyes,
Pretty well do I like your chin,
But much better did I love the little Massie Grove
Than you and all your kin, kin
Than you and all your kin."

This is a version of Child 81 "Little Musgrave and Lady Barnard," a ballad whose first notice is a reference in a play of 1613. It was also mentioned or quoted in several later seventeenth-century dramas. It has been widely sung and collected, being reported from folksingers in Maine, Missouri, North Carolina, Tennessee, South Carolina, Virginia, West Virginia, Ohio, Vermont, Kentucky, Michigan, and Oklahoma as well as in Newfoundland and Nova Scotia. It is known traditionally by numerous titles including "Lord Banner," "Lord Barney," "Lord Daniel," "Lord Darnell," "Lord Darnold," "Lord Valley," "Lord Vanover," "Lord Arnold's Wife," "Little Matthew Grove," "Little Mosie Grove," "Little Musgrave and Lady Narmwell," "The Red Rover," "Tomper's Song," "Mathey Grove," "Little Mathigrew," and "Lord Thomas," and the title used for the present version. There are four story types of the ballad as found in the United States, the first being that contained in the present text. The second type has the same story, but it is mentioned at the end that the Lord is to be hanged. A third story type has the same narrative minus the cajoling of the lover by the lady or refusal by Massie at the start. Upon seeing Massie embrace the lady, the page leaves. The final story type tells that the lord is to be hanged but at the beginning it is Lord Dannel who attends church one holiday where he learns of his wife's infidelity.

Because this ballad apparently exists in America purely by means of oral tradition (at least some scholars have assumed this to be the case) it has been seen as especially important in revealing how folksongs develop. Phillips Barry examined it for this purpose, concluding that there were two versions (one containing the bugle blowing and the "away, Musgrave, away" refrain, the other mentioning King Henry). He maintained that these split in Britain and developed independently in America. Barry further argued that the American texts are more vivid and incisive than Child's and probably older. Ultimately, he concluded that the song has been in this country over 300 years, i.e. since about 1630.

Barry's ideas, however, about a pre-American split have not been generally accepted.

American versions of the ballad begin either at church, at a ball, or while playing ball. Generally, southern American texts begin at church while northern ones begin while playing ball. Sometimes the lord regrets killing Massie and in a few American versions commits suicide. The lady is more aggressive in the United States than she is in English versions. American texts are also unlike Old World ones in that no past affair between the lovers is indicated.

The present version was collected October 25, 1976, by Kip Lornell from Ruby Bowman Plemmons, Meadows of Dan, Virginia. In 1932 she recorded the same ballad, and several others, for Arthur K. Davis of the University of Virginia. All of her songs were learned from her parents or friends but, for Davis, she admittedly refreshed her memory by going through a book of ballads. The present text is almost identical to that Plemmons supplied Davis, the single difference being in verse six where Davis's "a-laughin' and a-talkin' " becomes "huggin' and a-kissin'." This is, as Lornell correctly notes, evidence that for the ballad singer there is indeed a "correct" version; it is the one they have learned. Ballad scholars, of course, have traditionally maintained that all versions are equally "correct." Plemmons's version, although fifteen verses long, is a condensed version of the total narrative. The warning sent to Lord Darnold is omitted as is the two final killings found in many versions. Thus, the ending becomes tragic pathos rather than violence.

Little Rosewood Casket

In that little rosewood casket
That is resting on a marble stand;
Is a package of old letters
Written by a cherished hand.

Will you go and get them, sister,
Will you read them o'er to me;
For of' times I've tried to read them,
But for tears I could not see.

Read those precious lines so slowly
That I'll not miss even one;
For the cherished hand that wrote them,
His last work for me is done.

You have got them now, dear Sister,
Come and sit upon my bed;
And press gently to your bosom
This poor, throbbing, aching head.

Tell him that I never blamed him,
Though to me he proved untrue.
Tell that I'll ne'er forget him
Till I bid this world adieu.

Tell him I never blamed him,
Not an unkind word was spoke;
Tell, oh, tell him, Sister, tell him,
That my heart from his coldness broke.

When I'm dead and in my coffin,
And my shroud's around me bound;
And my little bed is ready
In the cold and silent ground,

Place his letters and his locket,
Both together o'er my heart,
But the little ring he gave me
From my finger never part.

You have finished now, dear Sister,
Will you read them o'er again;
While I listen to you read them
I will lose all sense of pain.

While I listen to you read them,
I will gently fall asleep;
Fall asleep to wake with Jesus;
Oh, dear Sister, do not weep.

In a little rosewood casket,
Resting on a marble stand,
There is a package of old letters,
Written by a cherished hand.

Go and bring them to me sister,
Read them o'er to me tonight,
I have often tried but could not,
For the tears would dim my sight.

Read them over gently sister,
While I'm lying upon my bed,
Pressing gently to your bosom
This aching troubled head.

Read them over gently sister,
And if I should fall asleep,
Fall asleep to wake with Jesus,
Dearest sister do not weep.

When I am dead and in my coffin,
And I am shrouded all around,
And my narrow bed is ready,
In that dear old churchyard ground.

Take his picture and his letters,
Place them nearest my heart,
For in life we loved each other,
And in death we must not part.

This nineteenth-century song not only has remained popular for over a century with traditional singers, but it is also interesting as an example of a song that is almost never known by its original title. It was a minor hit of 1870 under the title "A Package of Old Love Letters," the combined work of Louis P. Goullaud and Charles A. White. Little is known about Goullaud, but White was one of the more successful and prolific composers of his day. Born in Boston in 1830 he showed musical talent at a very early age and is said to have fashioned his first violin from a cigar-box. Nevertheless, White's first job was as an instructor at the Naval Academy in Newport, Rhode Island. Eventually he drifted into the music-publishing business; in 1869 he formed his own publishing house, an organization that is still in existence. A year before, in 1868,

Oliver Ditson published White's first national hit, "The Widow in the Cottage By the Seaside," a song destined to be widely plagiarized during the next thirty years.

In 1870 White had two hits in addition to "A Package of Old Love Letters"—"Come, Birdie, Come" and "Put Me In My Little Bed." In 1871 he scored again with "The Little Church Around the Corner" and "The Fisherman and His Child." Thereafter he produced at least one hit per year for the next twelve years. In terms of sheet music sales his greatest successes were "When the Leaves Begin to Turn" (1878), "A Bird From O'er the Sea" (1880), and "Marguerite" (1883). White remained active from 1883 until his death in 1892 but had no more big hits. His most successful numbers of this nine-year period were "President Cleveland's Victory March" (1884) and "My Love's a Rose" (1887).

Considering that White wrote hundreds of songs and had a large number of successes it is ironic that "A Package of Old Love Letters," a relatively minor effort of 1870 (minor in terms of sheet music sales), is the only one of his songs still commonly sung and hardly anyone associates the song with White. In fact, the editor of a recent folksong collection said the author and composer of "Little Rosewood Casket" are unknown. As far as the singers who pass the song along today are concerned, that is an accurate statement.

The first of the present versions was collected by Thomas D. Clark of Louisville, Mississippi from his mother, probably in the mid-1920s (the exact date is not given). Clark recorded this song and several others for a class at the University of Mississippi under Arthur Palmer Hudson. Clark later spent several years teaching history at the University of Kentucky and became noted for his several books such as *The Rampaging Frontier* (1939) and *The Southern Country Store* (1944). The second text was set down from memory by Ethel Clark of Louisville, Mississippi. She noted that she knew the tune but did not record it. Her collection was also done for Hudson's class at approximately the same time as Clark's.

126

Lonesome Scenes of Winter

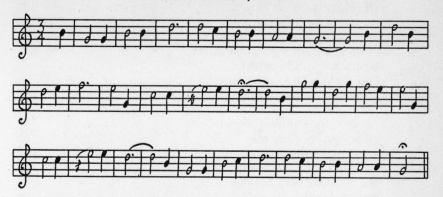

COLLECTED BY DIANNE DUGAW FROM LAWRENCE HIGHTOWER, CANAAN MOUNTAIN,
ARKANSAS, AUGUST, 1973. TRANSCRIPTION BY DIANNE DUGAW.

The lonesome scenes of winter
Confine with frost and snow.
Dark clouds around they gather
While chilly winds do blow.
You are the one I've chosen
To be my dearest dear.
Your scornful heart lies frozen,
Locked up in safely care.

Last night I went to see my love,
She treated me scornfully.
I asked if she would marry;
She would not answer me.
The night was far advancing
Toward the dawn of day.
My love, what is your answer?
My love, what do you say?

If an answer I must give you,
I choose the single life.
I never thought you worthy
Of calling me your wife.
So take this for your answer,
And call yourself replied,
I'm courting me another,
And you must stand aside.

Oh, if you are changing
The old now for the new,
I'll mount the little gray pony
And start to bid adieu.
I'll go and court some other maiden
Where love can have its fill.
This world is large and plenty;
There's lots of pretty girls still.

Oh, the little bird sang sweetly
All around on every tree.
Adieu to the world of pleasure.
This girl's gone back on me.
The little bird sang sweetly
On every bush and vine.
How freely would I give this whole world
If she were only mine.

In the course of six months longer
This maiden's mind hath changed.
She wrote this boy a letter
A-saying she was ashamed.
Since the time I slighted you,
Your name I cannot bear,
So here's my heart, love, take it
And keep it in your care.

He wrote her an answer,
He sent it back in speed.
I once loved you dearly,
I loved you then indeed.
Since that time you slighted me,
You pretty girl, never mind.
I'm courting me another,
So leave me to my find.

I told you when you slighted me
That I bid you a long farewell.
You can never expect to see me
Although I wish you well.
I told you when you slighted me,
This world were large and wide.
I'm courting me another lover,
Yes, she will stand by my side.

The origin of this ballad has not been determined but it is generally thought to be a native American effort despite its similarity to several British broadsides. G. Malcolm Laws assigns it number H12 in *Native American Balladry,* p. 236, classifying it under the heading "Ballads on Various Topics." Laws calls it "The Lonesome (Stormy) Scenes of Winter" and that is the title by which it is usually known. Other commonly encountered titles include "Chilly Scenes of Winter," "Dark Scenes of Winter," "Dread Scenes of Winter," and "Pretty Polly." The title "If One Won't Another One Will" used on a 1932 recording by the Carter Family seems to be used only by those singers imitating the Carter recording.

This song has been infrequently reported from oral tradition, being collected in Nova Scotia, Missouri, Kentucky, Georgia, Tennessee, and Arkansas. It has, however, been recorded commercially on several occasions, one of the most recent being on a Folkways album by Cousin Emmy (Cynthia Mae Carver) (1903–1980). Incidentally, Emmy, or the recording company, claimed to have written the song, but it is just an arrangement of the traditional ballad.

The version of "Lonesome Scenes of Winter" given here was collected in August, 1973 by Diane Dugaw from the singing of Lawrence Hightower, Canaan Mountain, Arkansas.

FROM THE SINGING OF DIANE WELDON AS RECORDED AT THE 1963 FLORIDA FOLK
FESTIVAL. TRANSCRIPTION BY W. K. McNEIL.

One day as I rambled
Down by the seashore,
The wind it did whistle,
The waves they did roar.
I spied a fair damsel
Make a pitiful cry,
It sounded so lonesome
In the waters nearby.

"I never will marry,
I'll be no man's wife.
I expect to live single
All the days of my life.
The shells in the ocean
Will be my deathbed:
The fish in deep waters
Swim over my head.

"My love's gone and left me,
He's the one I adore,
He's gone where I never
Will see him no more."
She plunged her fair body
In the waters so deep;
She closed her sad blue eyes,
In the water to sleep.

"I never will marry,
I'll be no man's wife.
I expect to live single
All the days of my life."

This ballad, which has been quite popular with folk revival performers, is probably derived from an eighteenth-century broadside
known as "The Sorrowful Ladie's Complaint" or "The Damsel's Lament."
Today, the latter or "The Maiden's Lament" is sometimes used, but
generally it is called "I Never Will Marry." Recordings by the Carter

Family and Texas Gladden, the latter a field recording for the Library of Congress, are largely responsible for the present popularity of this ballad. The folk revival group, The Weavers, popularized a version in the 1950s containing essentially the same melody as the present text but with the opening lines "They say that love is a funny thing." The text given here was recorded at the 1963 Florida Folk Festival from the singing of Diane Weldon, Gainesville, Florida. Diane was born in 1946 and learned her songs from her mother, Sybil Weldon, also of Gainesville. Like most versions of this ballad, the text known by the Weldons is short, containing only two verses and one-and-a-half choruses.

Mary on the Wild Moor

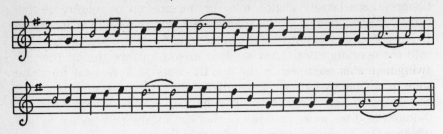

COLLECTED BY CHARLES W. JOYNER FROM MAE WESLEY MORSE, JEAN WESLEY DUSENBURY, AND JUNE WESLEY ELLIOTT, 1966–67, MURRELL'S INLET, SOUTH CAROLINA. TRANSCRIPTION BY CHARLES W. JOYNER.

One night when the winds blew cold
Blew bitter across the wild moor
Young Mary came with her child
Wandering home to her own father's door.

Oh, father please let me in,
Don't turn me away from your door.
The child at my bosom will die
From the winds that blow across the wild moor.

But the father was deaf to her cries,
Not the sound of her voice passed the door.
The watchdogs did bark but the winds
Grew bitter across the wild moor.

Oh, how must the father have felt
When he went to the door the next morn,
There he found Mary dead and the child
Fondly clasped in its dead mother's arms.

The child to the grave was soon borne,
The father in grief passed away.
The cottage to ruin has gone
And no one lives there to this day.

The villagers point out the spot
Where a willow droops over the door,
Where Mary perished and died
From the winds that blew across the wild moor.

Although this ballad is thought to have originated in a British broadside, its earliest known printing attributed to a specific person is a sheet music edition issued in Boston, circa 1845. This publication by Oliver Ditson, one of the most important music companies in nineteenth-century America, was credited to Joseph W. Turner, a then-successful popular song composer. Among Turner's other songs were "The Grave of Bonaparte" (1847), "The Silver Moon" (1848), "Thoughts at Twilight" (1858), and "Mother, When the War Is Over," most of which were published by Ditson. Although Turner did work with lyricists, the title page of the sheet music credits him with both words and music. This assertion, however, is not conclusive proof that Turner really was the song's creator, especially considering the rather lax copyright laws in existence at the time. Turner's claim may have been for the purpose of obtaining royalties on a song that was not his. Such a practice was certainly not unknown in nineteenth-century (or, for that matter, twentieth-century) pop music, for there are many songs for which several writers claimed credit and, presumably, also collected royalties. For example, between 1868–1883 at least five different American songwriters copyrighted "Cottage By the Sea" but it was actually originally an English song.

The word "moor" in the title is a point in favor of an English origin for the song. "Moor," referring to a tract of open wasteland usually covered with heather and often marshy or peaty, is widely used in the British Isles but rarely encountered in the United States. Of course, "moor" could have been used by some knowledgeable songwriter desirous of giving his song a British flavor. The question of the ballad's provenance is seemingly resolved by Helen Kendrick Johnson in *Our Familiar Songs and Those Who Made Them* (1889). She says on page 303 that the ballad is "a combination of old English words and music" whose popularity is due to Turner writing the lyrics and the tune. A problem with this assertion is that several of the English versions do not share the tune given in Johnson or in Turner's sheet music edition.

Regardless of who is responsible for the tune, it has generally received more praise than the words. For example, Alton C. Morris, on page 398 of *Folksongs of Florida* (1950), remarks, "The song is poor poetically. Its survival is, no doubt, dependent upon the plaintive beauty of the mournful tale to which has been added an air in keeping with its pathos." Whether Morris's opinion is shared by most folksingers is hard, if not impossible to tell, for the simple reason that no one has ever bothered to ask them whether the words or the melody are the reason why they keep the ballad alive. Probably, it is a combination of the two, although folklorists have generally accepted the idea that traditional singers remember ballads because of the story content. This view is not without some validity, but one suspects that folklorists have readily adopted the attitude because they have been more oriented towards texts than music. Whatever the case, though, there is no denying that the ballad usually known as "Mary of the Wild Moor" is and has been very popular, both in England and the United States. The list given in the notes section of this book of other collections in which the ballad is found is proof enough of its popularity.

The present version was collected in 1966–1967 by Charles W. Joyner from Mae Wesley Morse, Jean Wesley Dusenbury, and June Wesley Elliott, Murrell's Inlet, South Carolina. The three women are the daughters of Paul Herbert Wesley of Murrell's Inlet who sang the song for field collectors a generation ago.

Shadow of the Pines

COLLECTED BY KAY L. COTHRAN FROM GEORGE W. MITCHELL, THOMASTON, GEORGIA, DECEMBER 28, 1967. TRANSCRIPTION BY KAY L. COTHRAN.

We wandered in th' shadow of th' pines my love and I,
While th' wind was blowing softly from th' sea.
A sudden fitful darkness stole across the summer sky,
And a shadow came between my love and me.
Some hasty words were spoken and then almost unaware,
Hasty answers to unthinking anger led.
And our heartsick bitter longing and our weeping and our prayer,
Ne'er can make those false an' cruel words unsaid.

CHORUS:
Come back to me sweetheart, an' love me as before.
Come back to me sweetheart, an' leave me never more.
In life's dull pathway the sun no longer shines.
Come love and meet me in the shadow of the pines.

135

You took the ring I gave you, nor cast a glance at me,
As you hel' the jewel trinket in your hand.
You turned around an' cast it in the waters of th' sea,
Where th' waves were splashing idly on th' sand.
You went your way unheeding th' tears I could not hide.
You went your way an' not a word was said.
While my stubborn heart was breaking underneath its mask of pride,
An' th' pine trees sobbed in pity overhead.

CHORUS: (same as before)

I awake from bitter dreaming but to call aloud your name.
I sleep again to dream those dreams once more.
My stubborn pride has left me, I admit I was to blame.
Forgive me dear an' love me as before.
For the future is o'erclouded with the darkness of despair.
In th' sky of life love's sun no longer shines,
And I'd give the whole world gladly jus' to meet you there again,
Reunited in the shadow of the pines.

CHORUS: (same as before)

Little is known about the authorship and composition of this song. It was published in 1895 and credited to a Hattie Lummis and a G.O. Lang, about whom nothing more is known. Although the practice of publishing pre-existing material and claiming it as one's own was not unknown at the time there is no reason to doubt that Lummis and Lang were responsible for the song, as no prior printing is known. Undoubtedly the number had some degree of popularity in sheet music form (at the time sheet music sales were *the* indicator of success) but it was not among the top sellers of the 1890s. It seems clear that the commercial country music industry is largely responsible for the song being known today. It was widely recorded but the most influential 78s were by Kelly Harrell, Bradley Kincaid, and Gene Autry (who recorded it twice). In addition, Kincaid included it in one of his best-selling folios of country music.

The version presented here was collected by Kay L. Cothran from George W. Mitchell of Thomaston, Georgia, December 28, 1967. Mr. Mitchell also sang a version of "Daisy Deane" which is reprinted in the present volume. About "Shadow of the Pines" he said, "I learned that about sevendy-five 'r eighty years ago." He added, "I b'lieve it wuz by a, a Georgia girl, I'm not sure." Although Mitchell was uncertain about his ascription, it is possible that Lummis was a Georgian. Such a statement should not, however, be taken as definitive proof for frequently a person who merely sings a song is assigned credit for writing it by her audience.

Three Lovers

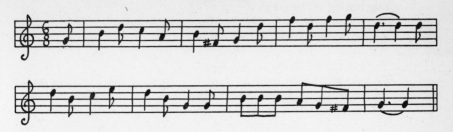

COLLECTED BY GEORGE FOSS FROM VIOLA COLE, FANCY GAP, VIRGINIA, 1962.
TRANSCRIPTION BY GEORGE FOSS.

Lord Thomas, he was a bold keeper,
The keeper of the king's deer,
Fair Ellender was a fair young lady,
Lord Thomas he loved her dear.

"Oh Mother, oh Mother come unriddle this sport,
Unriddle it all as one,
As to whether I should marry fair Ellender,
Or go bring the brown girl home."

"The brown girl she has house and land,
Fair Ellender has none,
Therefore I advise you as my best friend,
To go bring the brown girl home."

He rode unto Fair Ellender's house,
He tingled at the ring,
There was none so ready as Fair Ellender herself,
To rise and ask him in.

"What news, what news, Lord Thomas," she cried,
"What news you bring to me?"
"I've come to ask you to my wedding,
Is that good news to thee?"

"Bad news, bad news, Lord Thomas," she cried,
"Bad news you bring to me.
I thought I was to be your bride,
And you the bridegroom to be."

"Go saddle me up the milk-white horse,
Go saddle me up the brown,
Go saddle me up the swiftest horse,
That ever walked on ground."

137

She rode unto Lord Thomas's house,
She tingled at the ring,
There's none so ready as Lord Thomas himself,
To rise and ask her in.

He took her by the lily white hand,
He led her through the hall,
He led her to the head of the table,
Among the gentries all.

"Is this your bride, Lord Thomas?" she cried,
"She looks most wonderful brown,
When you could 'a' married as fair a young lady,
That ever the sun shone on."

The brown girl had a pen knife in her hand,
It looked most keen and sharp,
She pierced it through fair Ellender's side,
And it entered near her heart.

"What is the matter?" Lord Thomas, he cried,
"What is the matter?" cried he,
"Why don't you see my own heart's blood,
Come trinkling down by me?"

He took the brown girl by the hand,
He led her through the hall,
He took a sword and cut her head off,
And stoved it against the wall.

"Oh Mother, oh Mother, go make my grave,
Go make it wide and deep,
And bury fair Ellender in my arms,
And the brown girl at my feet."

He placed the sword against the ground,
The point against his breast,
Saying, "Here's the end of three young lovers,
God send them all to rest."

This is a version of another of the 305 ballads compiled by Child, his number 73, "Lord Thomas and Fair Annet." It is derived from a broadside common in the time of Charles II (1660–1685) that was licensed by L'Estrange, who was censor from 1663 to 1685. Samuel Pepys included it in his collection of broadsides which he completed in 1700, and a Scottish version appeared in Thomas Percy's *Reliques of Ancient English Poetry*

(1765). This story about a man who marries for riches rather than love has proven to be extremely popular in the United States but seems to be on the wane in Britain. Even so, it is, according to Bertrand Bronson, the second most popular of the Child ballads; only "Barbara Allen" enjoys greater favor. Even though the ballad is almost totally lacking in suspense or surprise the reasons for its popularity are evident. The narrative moves very quickly, being aided by explosive situations and melodrama of the most violent kind. The principal figures are lacking in emotional restraint, letting their passions rule their actions even to the point of leading them to commit the most brutal acts.

The ballad has been collected from all of the Southern states but Georgia and Lousiana as well as from Maine, Missouri, Indiana, West Virginia, New York, Ohio, Vermont, Michigan, Utah, Illinois, Nebraska, Pennsylvania, Iowa, Maryland, and Oklahoma. In addition it has also been reported from Newfoundland and Nova Scotia. "The Brown Girl" is the most popular of the various titles by which it is known; others include "The Brown Bride," "The Legend of Fair Eleanor and the Brown Girl," "Fair Ellen," "Fy Ellinore," "Lord Thomas's Wedding," "The Three True Lovers," "Parrot of Two Lovers," and that used for the present version. There is little variation in the narrative for only two story types are found in America. The first is the one given in the present text while the financial situation is reversed in the second story type; in other words the brown girl is poor and Fair Eleanor rich.

This ballad is very closely related to two others listed by Child, number 74 "Fair Margaret and Sweet William" and 75 "Lord Lovel." In "Lord Thomas and Fair Annet" a triangle results in three violent deaths, in 74 there is a triangle and two deaths while 75 has no triangle but does have two remorseful deaths. The rose-briar motif, also found in "Barbara Allen," frequently turns up in versions of the three ballads. In view of such similarities it is not surprising that verses from all three songs are frequently mingled together.

The present version was collected in 1962 by George Foss from Viola Cole, Fancy Gap, Virginia. In common with most American versions of this ballad, Cole's beginning differs from that of the Child texts which open with the two lovers sitting on a hill. Here, of course, the ballad starts with a description of Lord Thomas as a "bold forester."

Pretty Polly

COLLECTED SEPTEMBER 1, 1962 BY GEORGE FOSS FROM MAUD BOELYN, ARY, KENTUCKY. TRANSCRIPTION BY DAN BRACKIN.

"Pretty Polly, pretty Polly, come go along with me,
Pretty Polly, pretty Polly, come go along with me,
Before we get married some pleasure to see."

He led her over hills and valleys so deep,
He led her over hills and valleys so deep,
Till at length pretty Polly began for to weep.

"Oh Willie, oh Willie, I'm afraid of your ways,
Oh Willie, oh Willie, I'm afraid of your ways,
I'm afraid you are leading my body astray."

"Pretty Polly, pretty Polly, you're guessing just right,
Pretty Polly, pretty Polly, you're guessing just right,
For I've dug on your grave the most of last night."

They went on a piece further and what did they spy?
Went on a piece further and what did they spy?
A new dug grave and a spade lying by.

"Oh Willie, oh Willie, oh Willie, my dear,
Oh Willie, oh Willie, oh Willie, my dear,
How can you kill a poor girl that loves you so dear?"

She threw her arms around him and begged for her life,
She threw her arms around him and begged for her life,
Deep into her bosom he plunged the fatal knife.

He threw the dirt in on her and turned to go home,
He threw the dirt in on her and turned to go home,
Left nothing around but the poor birds to mourn.

This is a condensation of "The Gosport Tragedy, or the Perjured

Ship's Carpenter," a British broadside that dates back at least to 1750. It is one of many ballads sung in America about a man who murders his sweetheart, sometimes from jealousy but more often from a desire to be rid of her after getting her pregnant, and one of only two such songs that can definitely be traced back to a British broadside. Some versions of "Pretty Polly" contain some verses from "Knoxville Girl," the other American sweetheart-murder ballad derived from a British broadside, but the two can easily be distinguished because of certain story elements. In "Knoxville Girl" the killer explains the blood on his clothes by saying that it was caused by "bleeding at the nose." In "Pretty Polly" he tells the victim that he has been digging on her grave most of the previous evening. In most versions of "Pretty Polly" the reason for the murder is unstated, a situation that is often explained as being due to religious reasons. Possibly a religious conservatism that finds unwed pregnancies improper for public mention may be the reason for the omission but it is not the only probable explanation. It could simply represent a loss of detail in the process of oral transmission. There is also the possibility of intentional or unintentional editing to make "The Gosport Tragedy," a thirty-five quatrain ballad, into a shorter, more direct song. Whatever the case, the courtship, seduction, and pregnancy of the original ballad are left out altogether; instead the narrative focuses primarily on the murder itself which is treated almost casually as, for example, in the last verse.

The present ballad should not be confused with several other traditional songs known as "Pretty Polly," most of them being of the female warrior in disguise type. The present ballad is also known as "The Cruel Ship's Carpenter" and generally the murderer is unnamed. Whenever he does have a name, Willie is the one most commonly used. The present version of the ballad was collected September 1, 1962, by George Foss from Maud Boelyn, Ary, Kentucky. Mrs. Boelyn was born near Ary in 1897 and learned the songs she knew as a small girl from members of her family. She lived with her sister, Elizabeth Duff, who also learned the same songs as a girl around the turn of the century, and the two often corrected each other's ballad performances.

Ballads of Cowboys and Pioneers

The Disappointed Lover

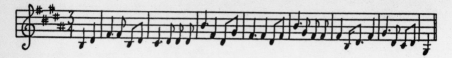

COLLECTED BY IRENE J. CARLISLE, MARCH 11, 1951 FROM DONEY HAMMONTREE,
BETHEL GROVE, ARKANSAS. TRANSCRIPTION BY DOROTHY OSWALD.

Early, early on one spring,
I stepped on board to serve my king,
And leave my dearest girl behind,
That often told me she were mine.

As she lay smiling in my arms
I thought her worth ten thousand charms,
With compliments and kisses sweet,
Saying, "We'll get married next time we meet."

One night while on the raging sea
I took an opportunity
To write unto my dearest dear,
But nothing from her could I hear.

I stepped into her father's hall,
And for my sweetheart I did call;
Her father made me this reply,
Saying, "She is married; you must be denied."

It's then I asked, "What did she mean?"
Her father answered in her name,
Saying, "She has married a richer life;
Go now, and choose you another wife."

It's cursed be to silver and gold,
And all fair maids that won't prove true;
They will their own fair promise break,
And marry another for riches' sake.

It's since I've lost my golden crown
I'll sail the ocean round and round.
I'll sail the sea till the day I die
And split the waves where the bullets fly.

"Oh, Willie, Willie, stay on shore;
Don't go to the raging sea any more;
There's girls in town truer than I;
Don't go to the war where the bullets fly."

"Rather be where the drums and the fife doth play,
Never ceasing night or day;
Rather sail the sea till the day I die
Than be in a false girl's company."

This American ballad is a greatly reworked adaptation of a seventeenth century British number "The Seaman's Complaint." It is known under various titles including "Early in the Spring," "Midnight on the Stormy Deep," and, most often, "The Trail to Mexico." It appeared fairly often on commercial country recordings. The version used here was collected by Irene J. Carlisle from Doney Hammontree, Bethel Grove, Arkansas, March 11, 1951. Hammontree had learned the ballad as a child from his own family.

Hammontree was born at Greenland, Arkansas, and later moved to Hog Eye, a small community about fifteen miles west of Fayetteville. For most of his adult life he lived at Bethel Grove. As a young man Hammontree attended several "singing schools," and learned some of his songs there. Most of his extensive repertoire, however, came from a blind man, Sam Beverly, who stayed with his family during the two years when Doney was seven to nine years old. Hammontree had a high, clear singing voice and a great interest in preserving folksongs and games. Several of the ballads he knew, such as "Dick German the Cobbler" were rare in American tradition.

The Dying Cowgirl

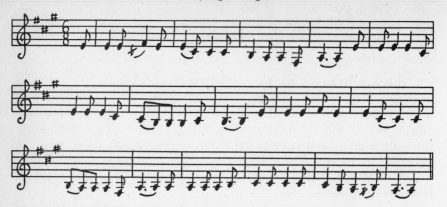

COLLECTED JULY, 1984 BY AN UNIDENTIFIED FIELDWORKER FOR THE FLORIDA FOLKLIFE PROGRAMS FROM LOUISE SANDERS, PERRY, FLORIDA. TRANSCRIPTION BY DREW BEISSWENGER.

I staked my claim out in the West when I was but a boy.
I was out there all alone, no happiness or joy.
I had to fight the Indians as over the plain they roamed.
Old Paint and I we just got back and called that place our home.

We started rustling cattle, just rounding up the strays.
In the saddle all the time, just riding night and day.
And in the stars we trusted them to guide us over the plains,
To guide us back to our old shack with four strays home again.

As I rode out from camp one night a storm was raging high,
The sound of hoofbeats caught my ear, I heard a human cry.
I sat up in my saddle, I turned Old Paint around,
I saw a dying cowgirl a-lying on the ground.

I knelt beside that dying girl, I tried to say a prayer.
I hoped that God in all his love could hear me pleading there.
I saw her blue eyes open, she smiled at me so sweet.
She said that she would wait for me up there where cowhands meet.

And now she sleeps out yonder, out on that lonely range,
Where all the stars watch over her until we meet again.

Although this ballad is similar in content to some other cowboy ballads reported from folk tradition it seems to be previously unreported. The story line seems to be incomplete although there is no indication that the singer forgot any words. Apparently, the protagonist and the girl had known each other prior to their accidental meeting on the plains, otherwise the story seems ludicrous. The ballad was collected in July, 1984 by an unidentified fieldworker for the Florida Folklife Programs from Louise Sanders, Perry, Florida. Sanders, who was seventy-two years old at the time of recording, learned her songs as a girl growing up in the southern Georgia town of Moultrie. She often sang with family and friends on the front porch or in the parlor where a pump organ was used for accompaniment. She has lived in several north Florida communities during the last fifty years, for the past few years at her current address in Perry.

The Indian Song

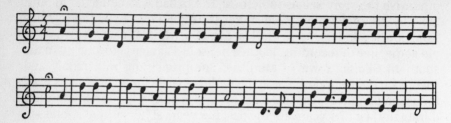

COLLECTED BY THOMAS G. BURTON, DECEMBER, 1965 FROM MRS. GRACE GOFORTH, KNOXVILLE, TENNESSEE. TRANSCRIPTION BY ANNETTE WOLFORD.

I'll sing you a song, it may be a sad one,
Of trials and troubles when first we begun;
Was leaving my country, my kindred, my home
To cross the wide plains of Wyoming to roam.

We crossed the Missouri, a jolly wide stream,
Which bears us so many those deserts and plains,
Hunting and fishing and searching for gold
And shooting flamingo and wild buffalo.

We traveled three weeks when we came to the flats;
We corralled our horses on the green, grassy flats;
We fixed up our tents on the green, grassy ground
While the mules and the horses were grazing around.

They talked of some Indians all over the plains,
Shooting their drivers and burning their trains;
They'd shoot those poor drivers with arrows and bows;
When captured by Indians, no mercy was shown.

While taking refreshments we heard a loud yell;
Was a whoop of some Indians came out on our trail.
We sprang to our rifles with a flash in each eye;
The captain said, "Brave boys, we'll fight till we die."

We mounted our horses, made ready to fight
When all of a sudden they came to our sight.
Our little band, just twenty and four,
And those of the Indians five hundred or more.

They came down upon us with a whoop and a yell;
At the crack of our rifles the twelve of them fell.
They saw their brave men lying dead on the ground;
They whooped and they yelled and they circled around.

Surrounded by Indians all over the plain,
It's enough to make the heart of any man faint,
But we fought them with courage and spoke not a word
Till the end of the battle was all that was heard.

We killed their brave chief at the head of his band;
He died like a soldier with his gun in his hand.
They saw their brave chief lying dead in his grave;
They whooped and they yelled and they circled away.

We hitched up our horses and started our train,
Had three more fights that trip on the plain,
And in our last battle three brave boys fell;
We laid them to rest on the green, grassy dell.

This ballad is sometimes known as "Crossing the Plains" or "The Indian Fighters" but is usually called "The Sioux Indians." Exactly when the song was written and by whom is unknown, and at this late date it is unlikely anyone will determine such matters. Certainly there is little doubt that the piece dates from the nineteenth century. In *American Murder Ballads and Their Stories* (1958), Olive Woolley Burt mentions a then-octogenarian, Sylvester Pierce of Gunnison, Utah, who recalled learning the song around the turn of the century when, presumably, it was already an old song. Pierce was also adamant that it was an autobiographical ballad although he could furnish no details other than his opinion. A version, probably contributed by a student, was included in the first edition of John Lomax's *Cowboy Songs and Other Frontier Ballads* (1910). Vance Randolph printed a text learned by Arthur Trail in Fayetteville, Arkansas, about 1906. Finally, it was one of the first songs discussed in Robert Winslow Gordon's column "Old Songs That Men Have Sung" which ran in *Adventure* magazine 1923–1927. In addition to these texts from Texas, Utah, Ohio, and Arkansas, the song has previously been reported from Colorado, Arizona, and Tennessee, although perhaps it is more widely known than its appearance in printed folksong collections indicates.

The present version was collected in December, 1965 by Thomas G. Burton from Mrs. Grace Goforth, Knoxville, Tennessee. No information is available about Mrs. Goforth other than she apparently had a large repertoire which, if the material recorded by Burton is indicative, consisted mainly of songs from the latter half of the nineteenth century. The overwhelming majority of Goforth's repertoire seems to be of native American origin.

John Henry

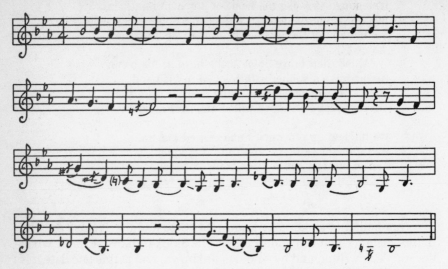

COLLECTED SEPTEMBER 17, 1977 BY KIP LORNELL FROM JOHN CEPHAS, BOWLING
GREEN, VIRGINIA. TRANSCRIPTION BY DREW BEISSWENGER.

John Henry was a little boy,
No bigger than the palm of your hand.
By the time that boy was nine years old,
He was driving spikes like a man.
Lord, Lord, driving spikes like a man.

Well now, John Henry was a little boy,
Sitting on his mammy's knee.
Well he picked up a hammer and a little bit of steel,
He said "This hammer goin' to be the death of me,
Lord, Lord, hammer goin' be the death of me."

Well now, John Henry said to the captain,
"Captain, you oughta see me swing.
I weigh forty-nine pounds from my hips on down,
And I love to hear that cold steel ring.
Lord, Lord, I love to hear that cold steel ring."

Well now, John Henry said to the captain,
"A man ain't nothing but a man.
But before I let this steam drill beat me down,
I'm goin' die with the hammer in my hand,
Lord, Lord, die with that hammer in my hand."

Well now, John Henry went to the tunnel and drive,
The steam drill was by his side.
Well now, John drove steel to the end of the tunnel,
He lay down that hammer and he died.
Lord, Lord, lay down that hammer, Lord he died.

Well now, John Henry went to the tunnel,
By that steam drill he did stand.
He beat that steam drill three inches down,
Lord, lay down that hammer and, Lord, he died.
Lord, Lord, lay down that hammer and he died.

Well now, John Henry had a little wife,
Her name was Polly Anne.
Well now, John got sick and he couldn't get well,
Polly drove steel like a man.
Lord, Lord, Polly drove steel like a man.

Well now, John Henry told the captain,
"Captain you ought to see me swing.
I weigh forty-nine pounds from my hips on down.
Lord, I love to hear that cold steel ring.
Lord, Lord, I love to hear that cold steel ring."

Well they took John Henry to the graveyard,
They buried him six feet in the sand.
Everytime a locomotive passed by,
They said that there lies a steel driving man,
Lord, Lord, there lies a steel driving man.

Well now, John Henry drove steel in the tunnel,
Till his hammer it caught on fire.
Well he looked at the water boy and he said,
"A cool drink of water 'fore I die,
Lord, Lord, cool drink of water 'fore I die."

Perhaps the most popular native American ballad is this story of a
black man's successful contest against a steam drill. Thought to describe
an actual event that occurred at the Big Bend Tunnel of the Chesapeake
and Ohio Railroad, nine miles east of Hinton, West Virginia sometime
around 1870–1872. The only problem is that no one has ever been able to
provide proof that the incident ever took place. The first published
reference to the ballad (other than broadsides) was in a 1909 *Journal of
American Folklore* article by Louise Rand Bascom. Since that time it has
appeared on numerous records, in several publications, and even in a

few movies. In short, as Richard Dorson demonstrated, the John Henry story has permeated every genre of American lore, from prose fiction to drama to art to stage musical. There have been two book-length studies of the John Henry tradition, one by Guy B. Johnson and the other by Louis W. Chappell. Neither book was based on primary historical documents for the simple reason that by the time Johnson and Chappell began their research C & O documents no longer existed. Some people believed that the C & O deliberately lost the documents because of the fear that they might cast the company in an unfavorable light owing to the poor working conditions tunnel drillers endured 1870–1872 at Big Bend Tunnel. Actually, despite a diligent search for such information, Chappell and Johnson could find no evidence that steam drills were even used at the Big Bend Tunnel.

It has generally been accepted that "John Henry" is set in West Virginia, but other locales have been proposed. The main ones generally offered are Kentucky, Alabama, and Jamaica. Both Chappell and Johnson dismissed the first two and Chappell also rejected the third one which was not discussed by Johnson. Basically, the other locales were dismissed not so much because the arguments for them were inherently weak but, rather, because of stronger evidence for the Big Bend Tunnel. It seems fair to note, though, that both men began their research predisposed in favor of the West Virginia site.

The John Henry ballads can be broken down into five basic parts. Of course, not all of these appear in every song but all are found frequently in the total song tradition. These elements include infantile premonition (while still a baby John Henry predicts the hammer will cause his death), preparation for the contest, the contest, his last testament, death, and burial, and some discussion of John Henry's woman. The latter part often includes some lines referring to her skill with the hammer and frequently recounts a dialogue between John Henry and his woman (in most texts named Polly Ann).

Usually "John Henry" is referred to as a Negro ballad but it is equally popular among whites. The author is anonymous but, according to Phillips Barry, was possibly white, because he was certainly influenced by white tradition. Barry based his conclusion on a Georgia broadside of c. 1900 attributed to a W. T. Blankenship who was white; on the similarity of some stanzas to those found in some versions of "Mary Hamilton," a Scottish ballad; and, finally, on the fact that the usual "John Henry" melody is a common tune of the British ballad "Earl Brand" (Child 7). Ultimately, though, Barry's assumptions about authorship are, like many of the "facts" concerning "John Henry," probably unprovable.

The present version was collected September 17, 1977 by Kip Lornell from John Cephas, Bowling Green, Virginia. Cephas (1931–) was born in

Bowling Green and still lives there on weekends while working in nearby Washington, D.C. during the week. He learned his music from local musicians and from records of performers as diverse as blues singer Blind Boy Fuller and country singer Louis Marshall "Grandpa" Jones. Cephas began playing guitar as a child and has recently gained a considerable reputation as a blues artist. He has been a featured performer on several tours in the United States and elsewhere. There is no indication of the source for his version of "John Henry."

Utah Carroll

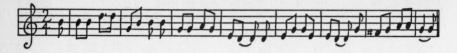

COLLECTED BY GEORGE FOSS FROM ALMEDA RIDDLE, PINE TOP, ARKANSAS, 1965.
TRANSCRIPTION BY GEORGE FOSS.

You ask me why, my little friend, I am so quiet and still;
And why a frown sits on my brow like a storm cloud on a hill.
Rein in your pony closer, I'll tell to you a tale
Of Utah Carroll, my partner, and his last ride on the trail.

In the land of Mexico in the place from whence I came,
In silence sleeps my partner in a grave without a name.
We rode the trail together and worked cows side by side,
Oh, I loved him like a brother, and I wept when Utah died.

We were rounding up one morning, our work was nearly done,
When off the cattle started on a wild frightened run.
Now the boss's little daughter was holding in that side.
She rushed to turn the cattle, 'twas there my partner died.

In the saddle of the pony where the boss's daughter sat,
Utah that very morning had placed a red blanket
That the saddle might be easier for his little friend,
But the blanket that he placed there brought my partner's life to an end.

When Leonora rushed in to turn the cattle, her pony gave a bound,
And the blanket slipped from beneath her and went trailing on the
    ground.
Now there's nothing on a cow ranch that will make the cattle fight
As quick as some red object would just within their sight.

When the cattle saw the blanket there trailing on the ground
They were maddened in a moment and they charged it with a bound.
When we cowboys saw what had happened, everyone just held our
    breath,
For if her pony failed her, none could save Leonora from death.

When Leonora saw the cattle, she quickly turned her face.
And leaned from out her saddle, caught the blanket back in place.
But in leaning lost her balance, fell before that maddened tide,
"Lie still, Leonora, I'm coming dear," were the words old Utah cried.

154

About fifteen yards behind her Utah came riding fast.
I little thought that moment that ride would be his last.
The horse approached the maiden with sure feet and steady bounds
And he leaned from out the saddle to catch her from the ground.

In falling from her pony, she dragged the blanket down,
And it lay there beside her where she lay upon the ground.
As he leaned to reach Leonora and to catch her in his arms
I thought my partner successful and Leonora safe from harm.

But such weight upon the cinches, they never had felt before,
His hind cinch burst asunder, and he fell beside Leonore.
Utah picked up the blanket, "Lie still again," he said.
And he ran across the prairie and waved the blanket over his head.

And thus he turned the cattle from Leonora his little friend,
And as the cattle rushed upon him, he turned to meet his end.
And quickly from his scabbard, Utah his pistol drew.
He was bound to fight while dying, like a cowboy brave and true.

His pistol flashed like lightning, the reports rang loud and clear,
As the cattle pinned down on him, he dropped the leading steer.
But they kept right on coming, my partner had to fall.
No more he will cinch the bronco or give the cattle call.

And when at last we reached him, there on the ground he lay,
With cuts and wounds and bruises, his life-blood oozing away.
Oh, I tell you what, little one, it was most awful hard,
I could not ride the distance in time to save my pard.

As I knelt down by him I knew his life was o'er,
But I heard him faintly murmur, "Lie still, I am coming, Leonora."
'Twas on one Sunday morning, I heard the parson say,
"I don't think your young partner will be lost on that great day."
He was just a poor young cowboy, maybe a little wild.
But God won't be too hard on a man who died to save a child.

This dramatic native American ballad was listed as B4 by G. Malcolm Laws in *Native American Balladry,* p. 135. While the story told here is not improbable it is generally believed that it is not based on any actual event. Exactly who wrote it is unknown but in *Cowboy Songs and Other Frontier Ballads,* John A. Lomax says that a J.T. Shirley of San Angelo, Texas claimed that a cowboy on the Curve T Ranch in Schleicher County was the author (p. 66). That cowboy's claim is not impossible but, without any other evidence, must be taken as doubtful. Frequently, someone who sings a song that his listeners haven't heard before is believed to be the person responsible for writing the piece. About all that can be said with certainty about the origins of this song is that it was written by some as yet unknown person sometime in the late nineteenth or early twentieth century.

Whatever the circumstances of "Utah Carl's" composition, there is no doubt about the persons responsible for popularizing the ballad with the general American public. Carl T. Sprague (1895–) grew up near Houston, Texas where he worked on his uncle's ranch; at the same time he learned a number of cowboy songs. Sprague eventually graduated from Texas A & M College and, from 1925–1934, he recorded thirty-two songs, mostly cowboy numbers, for commercially issued 78s. His first recording of "Utah Carroll" was on August 14, 1927 and, although not his biggest seller, did respectable business.

Perhaps more important than Sprague in popularizing "Utah Carl" with the general public was Ken Maynard (1895–1973). A native of Vevay, Indiana, Maynard was a champion rodeo rider and the first of the "singing cowboys" of the movies. He appeared in *The Wagon Master* in 1929 singing two traditional cowboy songs, and in 1933 in *The Strawberry Roan* he sang the title song. These are generally considered the first of the "singing cowboy" films. Moreover, Maynard received credit for introducing Gene Autry to the movies in his 1934 film, *In Old Santa Fe.* Not only in his movies but in various rodeo appearances Maynard performed "Utah Carroll" and similar songs.

"Utah Carl," "Utah Carroll," and "Utah Carl's Last Ride" are the titles most commonly used for the ballad. The ranchman's daughter is usually named Lenore, although in Ina Sires's *Songs of the Open Range,* pp. 6–7, she is called Vareo. The version given here was collected in 1965 by George Foss from Almeda Riddle, Pine Top, Arkansas. Riddle (1898–1986) was one of America's best known folksingers and Arkansas's most famous balladeer. Her repertoire was huge, reportedly consisting of as many as 600 songs, a small portion of which appear in *A Singer and Her Songs* (1970) and its forthcoming sequel, *Preserving Even the Scraps.* Many of Riddle's songs came from her father and older family members but this is one she learned from her children who may have had it from a record.

The Wandering Cowboy

COLLECTED MARCH 2, 1982 BY W. K. McNEIL FROM JIM McELROY, FOX, ARKANSAS.
TRANSCRIPTION BY DEE PATTERSON.

While lying on the prairie
One moonlight summer night,
Our heads upon our saddles
And campfires gleaming bright.

Some were telling stories,
A few were singing songs,
A few were idly smoking
As the hours rolled along.

At last we fell to talking
Of distant friends so dear,
A boy raised his head from the saddle
And he wiped away a tear.

The boy was young an' handsome,
His face wore a look of care,
His eyes were the color of heaven above
And he wore light wavy hair.

We asked him why he'd left his home,
Was his home so dear to him,
He hung his head for a moment,
With sadness his eyes grew dim.

At last he raised his head from his saddle,
And looked the rough crowd o'er,
He said, "Boys, I'll tell you the reason
Why I left old Kansas shore.

"I fell in love with a pretty little girl,
Her cheeks were soft an' white,
Well another fellow loved her too,
So it ended in a fight.

"In my dreams I can hear his voice
As he fell upon the ground.
He said, 'Bob, old boy, you'll be sorry
When you see me lyin' down.'

"I knelt to the bank beside him
To try and stop the blood
That flowed from his side
All in a crimson flood.

"So that's the reason why
That I'm compelled to roam,
A sinner of the darkest stain
Far far away from home."

No one knows who the author of "The Wandering Cowboy" is, so giving the exact date of its origin is impossible. Yet, there seems little reason to doubt that it originated during the years 1865–1885 that most historians consider the golden age of the cowboy. To my knowledge the earliest reported version is in Vance Randolph's *Ozark Folksongs,* collected in 1928 from Mrs. Lee Stephens of White Rock, Missouri. Mrs. Stephens claimed to have learned the song in McDonald County, Missouri, some thirty years earlier or, in other words, shortly before the turn of the century. It is probably safe to assume that the song was not new when Mrs. Stephens acquired it, for her source was another traditional singer. This information means that the song can definitely be traced back to the 1890s and probably slightly before that. Judging solely on the basis of stylistic considerations, it cannot have originated many years before the Civil War.

Like most folksongs this one has a number of titles by which it is known. The most common is "The Wandering Cowboy" but it is also known as "The Lone Star Ranger," "A Jolly Group of Cowboys," "Frenchman's Ranch," and "The Lonely Cowboy," among others. To date this piece has been collected by folklorists in Arizona, Arkansas, Missouri, North Carolina, and Texas but it may be much more widely known than this statistic indicates. Whatever current popularity "The Wandering Cowboy" has it is definitely not attributable to the influence of commercial recordings. To my knowledge it has appeared on less than half a dozen 78s and LPs, none of them being in any sense a best-selling item. It appears, then, that the song was written about 100 years ago by some, as yet, unidentified person and has remained alive all of this time mainly because of its popularity in folk tradition.

The version given here was recorded by W.K. McNeil from the singing of Jim McElroy of Fox, Arkansas, March 2, 1982. McElroy is a rancher and folksinger-poet who moved to Stone County in the early 1960s from his native New Mexico. Although he spends most of his time in the cattle business he has never lost his love of a good song or poem. He has also never given up writing verse himself and two of his poems, "Down in the Tules" (pronounced "Two-Lees") and "Outlaw Dunny," appeared in Glenn Ohrlin's *The Hell-Bound Train: A Cowboy Songbook* (1973). McElroy also still sings occasionally although not as much as he once did. Like many folksingers, McElroy did not give this song a title but merely referred to it as an old cowboy song.

Young Alban and Amandy

COLLECTED BY IRENE JONES CARLISLE, MARCH 21, 1951 FROM RACHEL HENRY, SPRING VALLEY, ARKANSAS. TRANSCRIPTION BY DOROTHY OSWALD.

The sun has gone down o'er the hills in the west,
And its last beams has faded o'er the mossy hill's crest;
Charms of beauty made nature so fair,
And Amandy was bound with her white bosom bare.

At the foot of the mountain,
Where Amandy did sigh
At the hooting of an owl,
Or a catamount cry,
Or the howl of some wolf
In its low granite cell,
Or the scrash of some tall
Forest tree as it fell.

Amandy was there,
All friendless and forlorn,
With her face bathed in blood
And her garments all torn.
It was vengeance she counted
In the eyes of her hoe
And sighed for the time
When her suffering might close.

It was out in the forest,
Where the wild games had flown,
And in its branches
Where the rude hammock swung.
War and plunder
Each warrior repose
From the dawn of the morning
Till evening had closed.

The campfires were kindled;
Each warrior was there,
And Amandy was bound
With her white bosom bare.
All around stood
The unmerciful throng,
Awaiting in patience
For the war dance and song.

Young Alban, the leader,
On the scenes did appear,
With an eye like an eagle
And a step like a deer,
Saying, "Forbear!
Your tortures forbear!
You shall live, by the war-whoop,
And that I'll swear.

"It's this maiden's freedom
That I do crave;
Give a sigh for her suffering
And a tear for her grave.
And tonight if your victim
Be burned by a tree,
Young Alban, your leader,
Your victim shall be."

The next morning was seen
A streak of red, white, and blue,
A-gliding o'er the waters
In a light bark canoe.
Like a wild dove
Sails over the tide,
Young Alban and Amandy
Together did ride.

The same morning was seen
A streak of red, white, and green,
O'er the blue bubbling waters
By the willow so green;
Brace was her joy
When she stepped on the shore,
To embrace her old father
And mother once more.

Young Alban he stood by
And saw the embrace,
With a sigh from his heart
And a tear on his face,
Saying, "All I ask
Is friendship and food
From the parents of Amandy
To the chief of the wood."

This ballad has been collected from Maine to Florida and as far west as Utah. It was written by the Reverend Thomas C. Upham, later Professor of Moral Philosophy at Bowdoin College, and first printed in the *Columbian Sentinel* (Boston), September 19, 1818. According to a W.A. Martin of Wellington, Colorado who wrote Otto Rayburn, at the time editor and publisher of the *Arcadian Magazine,* the song was based on two incidents, one history and the other fiction. Martin's theory held that "Alban" was a young Pawnee brave named Petalasharo who actually rescued a young girl from torture by his tribe. In gratitude, the young ladies of Miss White's school in Washington sent the young chief a silver medal, this incident occurring in 1821. Martin added that a further basis for the ballad is in James Fenimore Cooper's fictional story, "Wish-Ton-Wish" (See *Arcadian Magazine,* June, 1932, p. 4). Because Upham's poem "The White Captive" was published before either Cooper's story appeared or Petalasharo rescued the girl, it is impossible that either incident had anything to do with the ballad's origin. It is, however, very likely that both contributed to the song's popularity.

"Young Alban and Amandy," the title given by Rachel Henry, is unique. More commonly the ballad is known by its original title "The White Captive" but is also known as "Olban or Alban," "Her White Bosom Bare," "Amanda, the Captive," and "The Chief of the Utes." According to Phillips Barry (*The Maine Woods Songster,* p. 98) the song has only one authentic detail, the mention of a red meteor. Irene J. Carlisle, collector of the present version, thought the "streak of red, white, and green" in the ninth stanza of Henry's version to be "the stubborn survival of that meteor."

Rachel Henry spent her entire life near Springdale, Arkansas. She was born at nearby Brush Creek and, at the time of collection, was in her seventies.

The Young Man Who Wouldn't Hoe Corn

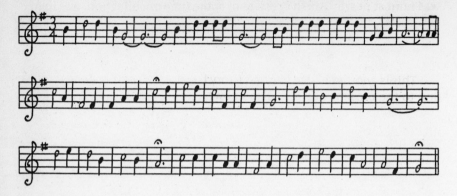

COLLECTED BY DIANNE DUGAW FROM LAWRENCE HIGHTOWER, BEE BRANCH,
ARKANSAS, AUGUST, 1973. TRANSCRIPTION BY DIANNE DUGAW.

Come all young people, and listen to my song.
I'll tell you of a young man who wouldn't hoe his corn.
For the reason why, I never could tell,
For this young man were always well.

In July, his corn knee-high,
In August he laid it by.
In September it came a Jack Frost,
And all this young man's corn was lost.

He goes to the fence, and he brings in
The weeds and the cockleburrs up to his chin.
The weeds and the careless grew so high,
It made that young man weep and cry.

He goes to the nearest neighbor's house,
A-courting as you might surmise.
Her suspicion had begun,
She said young man, have you hoed your corn?

He answered her with a sweet reply,
Oh yes, my love, I've laid it by.
But there isn't any use for me to complain,
For I don't believe I'll make a grain.

If you don't believe you'll make your bread,
What makes you try so hard to wed?
Single I am, and single I'll remain;
A lazy man I won't maintain.

So now he's gone to see a young widder,
And I hope to the Lord that he can't get her,
For a rake or a hoe or the handle of a plow
Is suiting him better than a wife for now.

This is another ballad whose history has not yet been traced. In addition to the present title it is also known as "The Lazy Man," "The Lazy Young Man," and "Harm [Hiram?] Link." It has been widely reported from tradition in the United States, versions being collected in Vermont, Missouri, West Virginia, Tennessee, Mississippi, Indiana, Iowa, Nebraska, North Carolina, Ohio, Texas, and Arkansas. Frequent collection in America and the lack of reports from other countries seem to indicate a native American product. In *Folk Song U. S. A.* (p. 223), Alan Lomax suggests that the ballad originated in New England or the Southeastern states from which it was carried westward by those who settled the frontiers of the Middle West. This thesis is, of course, plausible but is also pure speculation.

The present version of the song was collected August, 1973 in Bee Branch, Arkansas by Diane Dugaw from the singing of Lawrence Hightower. The informant accompanied himself on guitar.

PROPERTY OF
HIGH POINT PUBLIC LIBRARY
HIGH POINT, NORTH CAROLINA

Notes

Biblio-Discography

This biblio-discography is arranged in four sections: A. Basic references, B. Other references, C. 78 rpm records, and D. LP recordings. Section A consists of those books often cited in these notes, each volume being coded by a keyword. Usually a partial or complete (generally the latter) text appears on the pages cited. A full listing of these publications is given following these prefatory remarks; they are preceded by their keyword. Section B consists of printed references not in section A; these may be studies of individual songs or collections. Section C includes 78 albums as well as individual records, and section D includes both new releases and reissues of 78 rpm records. None of the sections should be construed as exhaustive lists of either publications or records dealing with an individual song. Instead, they are merely intended as a representative sampling of what is available; in most cases the listed items could be greatly increased. Where nothing appears under a numbered section that means I was unable to locate any relevant items in that category for the specific song.

Basic References

Abrahams & Foss	Abrahams, Roger D. and George Foss. *Anglo-American Folksong Style.* Englewood Cliffs, New Jersey: Prentice-Hall, Inc., 1968.
Abrahams & Riddle	Abrahams, Roger D. *A Singer and Her Songs: Almeda Riddle's Book of Ballads.* Baton Rouge: Louisiana State University Press, 1970.
Allen	Allen, Jules Verne. *Cowboy Lore.* San Antonio: The Naylor Printing Co., 1933.
Arnold	Arnold, Byron. *Folksongs of Alabama.* University: University of Alabama Press, 1950.
Barry	Barry, Phillips, Fannie Hardy Eckstorm, and Mary W. Smyth. *British Ballads from Maine.* New Haven: Yale University Press, 1929.
Belden	Belden, Henry M. *Ballads and Songs Collected by the Missouri Folk-Lore Society.* 1940. 2nd ed. Columbia: University of Missouri Press, 1955.

Boette   Boette, Marie. *Singa Hipsy Doodle and Other Folk Songs of West Virginia*. Parsons, West Virginia: McClain Printing Co., 1971.

Botkin   Botkin, Benjamin A. *A Treasury of American Folklore: Stories, Ballads, and Traditions of the People*. New York: Crown Publishers, 1944.

Botkin (1949)   Botkin, Benjamin A. *A Treasury of Southern Folklore*. New York: Crown Publishers, 1949.

Brewster   Brewster, Paul G. *Ballads and Songs of Indiana*. 1940. New York: Folklorica, 1981.

Bronson   Bronson, Bertrand H. *The Singing Tradition of Child's Popular Ballads*. Princeton: Princeton University Press, 1976.

Brown II   *The Frank C. Brown Collection of North Carolina Folklore. Volume 2, Folk Ballads*. Edited by Henry M. Belden and Arthur Palmer Hudson. Durham: Duke University Press, 1952.

Brown IV   *The Frank C. Brown Collection of North Carolina Folklore. Volume 4. The Music of the Ballads*. Edited by Jan Philip Schinhan. Durham: Duke University Press, 1962.

Browne   Browne, Ray B. *The Alabama Folk Lyric: A Study in Origins and Media of Dissemination*. Bowling Green, Ohio: Bowling Green University Popular Press, 1979.

Burt   Burt, Olive Woolley. *American Murder Ballads and Their Stories*. New York: Oxford University Press, 1958.

Burton & Manning I   Burton, Thomas G. and Ambrose N. Manning. *East Tennessee State University Collection of Folklore: Folksongs*. Johnson City: East Tennessee State University, 1967.

Burton & Manning II   Burton, Thomas G. and Ambrose N. Manning. *East Tennessee State University Collection of Folklore. Volume 2. Folksongs*. Johnson City: East Tennessee State University, 1969.

Bush I   Bush, Michael E. *Folk Songs of Central West Virginia*. Ravenswood, West Virginia: Custom Printing, 1969.

Bush II   Bush, Michael E. *Folk Songs of Central West Virginia*. Ravenswood, West Virginia: Custom Printing, 1970.

Cambiaire   Cambiaire, Celestin Pierre. *East Tennessee and Western Virginia Mountain Ballads*. London: The Mitre Press, 1934.

Carey   Carey, George G. *Maryland Folk Legends and Folk Songs*. Cambridge, Maryland: Tidewater Publishers, 1971.

Cazden   Cazden, Norman. *The Abelard Folksong Book*. New York: Abelard-Schuman, 1958.

Chappell   Chappell, Louis W. *Folk-Songs of Roanoke and the Albemarle*. Morgantown, West Virginia: Ballad Press, 1939.

Chase   Chase, Richard. *American Folk Tales and Songs*. New York: The New American Library of World Literature, Inc., 1956.

Cohen & Seeger   Cohen, John and Mike Seeger. *The New Lost City Ramblers Song Book*. New York: Oak Publications, 1964.

Cohen, N.   Cohen, Norm. *Long Steel Rail: The Railroad in American Folksong*. Urbana: University of Illinois Press, 1981.

Combs & Wilgus	Combs, Josiah H. *Folk-Songs of the Southern United States.* Edited by D. K. Wilgus. Austin: University of Texas Press, 1967.
Cox	Cox, John Harrington. *Folk-Songs of the South.* 1925. Reprint, New York: Dover Publications, Inc., 1967.
Creighton (1971)	Creighton, Helen. *Folksongs from Southern New Brunswick.* Ottawa: National Museum of Canada, 1971.
Creighton (1962)	Creighton, Helen. *Maritime Folk Songs.* Toronto: Ryerson Press, 1962.
Creighton & Senior	Creighton, Helen and Doreen H. Senior. *Traditional Songs from Nova Scotia.* Toronto: Ryerson Press, 1950.
Cutting	Cutting, Edith. *Lore of an Adirondack County.* Ithaca, New York: Cornell University Press, 1943.
Davis (1929)	Davis, Arthur Kyle, Jr. *Traditional Ballads of Virginia.* Cambridge: Harvard University Press, 1929.
Davis (1949)	_____ . *Folk Songs of Virginia: A Descriptive Index and Classification.* Durham: Duke University Press, 1949.
Davis (1960)	_____ . *More Traditional Ballads of Virginia: Collected with the Cooperation of Members of the Virginia Folklore Society.* Chapel Hill: University of North Carolina Press, 1960.
Dean	Dean, Michael C. *The Flying Cloud and One Hundred and Fifty Other Old Time Songs and Ballads.* Virginia, Minnesota: The Quickprint, 1922.
Downes & Siegmeister	Downes, Olin and Elie Siegmeister. *A Treasury of American Song.* New York: Alfred A. Knopf, Inc., 1943.
Eddy	Eddy, Mary Olive. *Ballads and Songs From Ohio.* 1939. Reprint, Hatboro, Pennsylvania: Folklore Associates, 1964.
Emrich (1972)	Emrich, Duncan. *Folklore on the American Land.* Boston: Little, Brown and Company, 1972.
Emrich (1974)	_____ . *American Folk Poetry: An Anthology.* Boston: Little, Brown and Company, 1974.
Fauset	Fauset, Arthur Huff. *Folklore from Nova Scotia.* New York: American Folklore Society, 1931.
Fife & Fife	Fife, Austin E. and Alta S. Fife. *Cowboy and Western Songs.* New York: Clarkson N. Potter, 1969.
Finger	Finger, Charles J. *Frontier Ballads.* Garden City, New York: Doubleday, Page, 1927.
Flanders	Flanders, Helen Hartness. *Ancient Ballads Traditionally Sung in New England.* Philadelphia: University of Pennsylvania Press, 1960. 4 volumes.
Flanders & Olney	_____ , and Marguerite Olney. *Ballads Migrant in New England.* New York: Farrar, Straus, and Young, 1953.
Fowke	Fowke, Edith. *Traditional Singers and Songs From Ontario.* Hatboro, Pennsylvania: Folklore Associates, 1965.
Fowke & Johnston	_____ , and Richard Johnston. *More Folk Songs of Canada.* Waterloo, Ontario: Waterloo Music Company, 1967.
Fuson	Fuson, Henry H. *Ballads of the Kentucky Highlands.* London: The Mitre Press, 1931.
Gainer	Gainer, Patrick. *Folk Songs from the West Virginia Hills.* Grantsville, West Virginia: Seneca Books, 1975.
Gardner & Chickering	Gardner, Emelyn E. and Geraldine Jencks Chickering.

	Ballads and Songs of Southern Michigan. 1939. Reprint, Hatboro, Pennsylvania: Folklore Associates, 1967.
Greenleaf & Mansfield	Greenleaf, Elisabeth Bristol and Grace Yarrow Mansfield. *Ballads and Sea Songs of Newfoundland.* Cambridge: Harvard University Press, 1933.
Grover	Grover, Carrie B. *A Heritage of Songs.* Edited by Anne L. Griggs. Norwood, Pennsylvania: Norwood Editions, n. d.
Heart	*Heart Songs Dear to the American People.* New York: World Syndicate Company, 1909.
Henry (1934)	Henry, Mellinger E. *Songs Sung in the Southern Appalachians.* London: The Mitre Press, 1934.
Henry (1938)	_____ . *Folk-Songs from the Southern Highlands.* New York: J. J. Augustin, 1938.
Henry & Matteson	_____ ; and Maurice Matteson. *Twenty-nine Beech Mountain Folk Songs and Ballads.* New York: G. Schirmer, 1936.
High	High, Fred. *Old, Old Folk Songs.* Berryville, Arkansas: no publisher or date of publication given.
Hubbard	Hubbard, Lester A. *Ballads and Songs from Utah.* Salt Lake City: University of Utah Press, 1961.
Hudson	Hudson, Arthur Palmer. *Folk-Songs of Mississippi and Their Background.* 1936. Reprint, New York: Folklorica, 1981.
Ives	Ives, Burl. *The Burl Ives Song Book: American Song in Historical Perspective.* New York: Ballantine Books, 1963.
Jameson	Jameson, Gladys V. *Sweet Rivers of Song: Authentic Ballads Hymns, Folksongs from the Appalachian Region.* Berea, Kentucky: Berea College, 1967.
Jekyll	Jekyll, Walter. *Jamaican Song and Story: Annancy Stories. Digging Sings, Ring Tunes, and Dancing Tunes.* 1907. Reprint, New York: Dover Publications, Inc., 1966.
Jones (1980)	Jones, Loyal. *Radio's 'Kentucky Mountain Boy' Bradley Kincaid.* Berea, Kentucky; Berea College Appalachian Center, 1980.
Jones (1984)	_____ . *Minstrel of the Appalachians: The Story of Bascom Lamar Lunsford.* Boone, North Carolina: Appalachian Consortium Press, 1984.
Joyner	Joyner, Charles W. *Folk Song in South Carolina.* Columbia: University of South Carolina Press, 1971.
Kennedy	Kennedy, Charles O'Brien. *American Ballads: Folk Treasures of the American Past in Verse and Song.* Greenwich, Connecticut: Fawcett Publications, Inc., 1952.
Killion & Waller	Killian, Ronald G. and Charles T. Waller. *A Treasury of Georgia Folklore.* Atlanta: Cherokee Publishing Company, 1972.
Larkin	Larkin, Margaret. *Singing Cowboy.* 1931. Reprint, New York: Oak Publications, 1963.
Leach	Leach, MacEdward. *The Ballad Book.* 1955. Reprint, New York; A. S. Barnes & Company, Inc., n. d.
Leisy	Leisy, James F. *The Folk Song Abecedary.* New York: Bonanza Books, 1966.
Lingenfelter	Lingenfelter, Richard E., Richard A. Dwyer, and David Cohen. *Songs of the American West.* Berkeley: University of California Press, 1968.

Linscott	Linscott, Eloise Hubbard. *Folk Songs of Old New England.* New York: Macmillan, 1939.
Lomax, A.	Lomax, Alan. *The Folk Songs of North America.* Garden City, New York: Doubleday, 1960.
Lomax, J.	Lomax, John A. *Adventures of a Ballad Hunter.* New York: Macmillan, 1947.
Lomax & Lomax	Lomax, John A. and Alan Lomax. *Cowboy Songs and Other Frontier Ballads.* Revised edition. New York: Macmillan, 1938.
MacColl & Seeger	MacColl, Ewan and Peggy Seeger. *Travellers' Songs From England and Scotland.* Knoxville: The University of Tennessee Press, 1977.
MacIntosh	MacIntosh, David S. *Folk Songs and Singing Games of the Illinois Ozarks.* Edited by Dale R. Whiteside. Carbondale: Southern Illinois University Press, 1974.
MacKenzie (1919)	MacKenzie, W. Roy. *The Quest of the Ballad.* Princeton, New Jersey: Princeton University Press, 1919.
MacKenzie (1928)	_____ . *Ballads and Sea Songs from Nova Scotia.* 1928. Reprint, Hatboro, Pennsylvania: Folklore Associates, 1963.
McGill	McGill, Josephine. *Folk-Songs of the Kentucky Mountains.* New York: Boosey, 1917.
Manny & Wilson	Manny, Louise and James Reginald Wilson. *Songs of Miramichi.* Fredericton, New Brunswick: Brunswick Press, 1968.
Moore & Moore	Moore, Ethel and Chauncy O. Moore. *Ballads and Folk Songs of the Southwest.* Norman: University of Oklahoma Press, 1964.
Morris	Morris, Alton C. *Folksongs of Florida.* 1950. Reprint, New York: Folklorica, 1981.
Munch	Munch, Peter A. *The Song Tradition of Tristan da Cunha.* Bloomington: Indiana University Research Center for the Language Sciences, 1970.
Neely	Neely, Charles. *Tales and Songs of Southern Illinois.* Edited by John W. Spargo. Menasha, Wisconsin: George Banta Publishing, 1938.
Niles I	Niles, John Jacob. *The Anglo-American Ballad Study Book.* New York: G. Schirmer, n. d.
Niles II	_____ . *More Songs of the Hill Folk.* New York: G. Schirmer, 1936.
Ohrlin	Ohrlin, Glenn. *The Hell-Bound Train: A Cowboy Songbook.* Urbana: University of Illinois Press, 1973.
Ord	Ord, John. *The Bothy Songs and Ballads of Aberdeen, Banff & Moray, Angus and the Mearns.* Paisley, Scotland: A. Gardner, 1930.
Owens (1950)	Owens, William A. *Texas Folk Songs.* Dallas: Southern Methodist University Press, 1950.
Owens (1983)	_____ . *Tell Me a Story, Sing Me a Song: A Texas Chronicle.* Austin: University of Texas Press, 1983.
Palmer	Palmer, Roy. *Everyman's Book of British Ballads.* London: J. M. Dent & Sons Ltd., 1980.
Parler	Parler, Mary Celestia. *An Arkansas Ballet Book.* Norwood, Pennsylvania: Norwood Editions, 1975.

171

Parsons (1918)   Parsons, Elsie Clews. *Folk Tales of the Andros Islands*. New York: American Folklore Society, 1918.

Parsons (1923)   ————. *Folklore of the Sea Islands*. New York: American Folklore Society, 1923.

Peacock   Peacock, Kenneth. *Songs of the Newfoundland Outports*. 3 volumes. Ottawa: National Museum of Canada, 1965.

Peters   Peters, Harry B. *Folk Songs Out of Wisconsin*. Madison: State Historical Society of Wisconsin, 1977.

Pound   Pound, Louise. *American Ballads and Songs*. 1922. Reprint, New York: Charles Scribner's Sons, 1972.

Raim & Dunson   Raim, Ethel and Josh Dunson. *Grass Roots Harmony*. New York: Oak Publications, 1968.

Raine   Raine, James Watt. *The Land of Saddle-bags*. New York: Council of Women for Home Missions and Missionary Education Movement of the United States and Canada, 1924.

Rainey   Rainey, Leo. *Songs of the Ozark Folk*. 2nd edition. Branson, Missouri: The Ozarks Mountaineer, 1976.

Randolph I   Randolph, Vance. *The Ozarks: An American Survival of Primitive Society*. New York: Vanguard Press, 1931.

Randolph II   ————. *Ozark Mountain Folks*. New York: Vanguard Press, 1932.

Randolph III   ————. *Ozark Folksongs*. 1946–1950. Reprint, Columbia: University of Missouri Press, 1980. 4 volumes.

Randolph & Cohen   ————, and Norm Cohen. *Ozark Folksongs*. 1 volume abridgement. Urbana: University of Illinois Press, 1982.

Rayburn   Rayburn, Otto Ernest. *Ozark Country*. New York: Duell, Sloan & Pearce, 1941.

Ritchie (1955)   Ritchie, Jean. *Singing Family of the Cumberlands*. 1955. Reprint, New York: Oak Publications, 1963.

Ritchie (1965)   ————. *Folk Songs of the Southern Appalachians as Sung by Jean Ritchie*. New York: Oak Publications, 1965.

Roberts (1974)   Roberts, Leonard. *Sang Branch Settlers: Folksongs and Tales of a Kentucky Mountain Family*. Austin: University of Texas Press, 1974.

Roberts (1978)   ————. *In the Pine: Selected Kentucky Folksongs*. Pikeville, Kentucky: Pikeville College Press, 1978.

Rosenberg   Rosenberg, Bruce A. *The Folksongs of Virginia: A Checklist of the WPA Holdings, Alderman Library. University of Virginia*. Charlottesville: University of Virginia Press, 1969.

Sandburg   Sandburg, Carl. *The American Songbag*. New York: Harcourt, Brace, 1927.

Scarborough (1925)   Scarborough, Dorothy. *On the Trail of Negro Folk-Songs*. 1925. Reprint, Hatboro, Pennsylvania: Folklore Associates, 1963.

Scarborough (1937)   ————. *A Song Catcher in Southern Mountains: American Folk Songs of British Ancestry*. New York: Columbia University Press, 1937.

Scott   Scott, John Anthony. *The Ballad of America: The History of the United States in Song and Story*. New York: Bantam Books, Inc., 1966.

Seeger	Seeger, Pete. *American Favorite Ballads*. New York: Oak Publications, 1961.
Sharp	Sharp, Cecil J. and Maud Karpeles. *English Folk-Songs from the Southern Appalachians*. 2 volumes. London: Oxford University Press, 1932.
Shellans	Shellans, Herbert. *Folk Songs of the Blue Ridge Mounains*. New York: Oak Publications, 1968.
Shoemaker (1923)	Shoemaker, Henry W. *North Pennsylvania Minstrelsy*. Altoona: Times Tribune, 1923.
Shoemaker (1931)	_____ . *Mountain Minstrelsy of Pennsylvania*. Philadelphia: Newman F. McGirr, 1931.
Smith	Smith, Reed. *South Carolina Ballads, with a Study of the Traditional Ballad Today*. Cambridge: Harvard University Press, 1928.
Smith & Rufty	_____ , and Hilton Rufty. *American Anthology of Old World Ballads*. New York: J. Fischer & Brothers, 1937.
Spaeth	Spaeth, Sigmund. *Read 'em and Weep: The Songs You Forgot to Remember*. Garden City, New York: Doubleday, Page, 1926.
Stout	Stout, Earl J. *Folklore from Iowa*. New York: American Folklore Society, 1936.
Sturgis & Hughes	Sturgis, Edith B. and Robert Hughes. *Songs from the Hills of Vermont*. New York: G. Schirmer, 1919.
Sulzer	Sulzer, Elmer G. *Twenty-Five Kentucky Folk Ballads*. Lexington, Kentucky: Transylvania Press, 1936.
Talley	Talley, Thomas W. *Negro Folk Hymns*. 1922. Reprint, Port Washington, New York: Kennikat Press, Inc., 1968.
Thomas (1931)	Thomas, Jean. *Devil's Ditties*. 1931. Reprint, Detroit: Gale Research Company, 1976.
Thomas (1939)	_____ . *Ballad Makin' in the Mountains of Kentucky*. 1939. Reprint, New York: Oak Publications, Inc., 1964.
Thomas & Leeder	_____ , and Joseph A. Leeder. *The Singin' Gatherin'!* New York: Silver Burdett Co., 1939.
Thompson	Thompson, Harold W. *Body, Boots and Britches: Folktales, Ballads and Speech from Country New York*. 1940. Reprint, Syracuse: Syracuse University Press, 1979.
Thompson & Cutting	_____ , and Edith E. Cutting. *A Pioneer Songster: Texts From the Stevens-Douglass Manuscript of Western New York 1841–1856*. Ithaca, New York: Cornell University Press, 1958.
Thorp	Thorp, N. Howard "Jack". *Songs of the Cowboys*. 1921. Reprint, Lincoln, Nebraska: University of Nebraska Press, 1984.
Warner	Warner, Anne. *Traditional American Folk Songs from the Anne & Frank Warner Collection*. Syracuse: Syracuse University Press, 1984.
Wells	Wells, Evelyn Kendrick. *The Ballad Tree*. New York: Ronald Press, 1950.
Wheeler	Wheeler, Mary. *Kentucky Mountain Folk Songs*. Boston: The Boston Music Company, 1937.
White	White, Newman Ivey. *American Negro Folk-Songs*. 1928. Reprint, Hatboro, Pennsylvania: Folklore Associates, 1965.

Williams   Williams, Alfred. *Folk-Songs of the Upper Thames.* London: Duckworth, 1923.

Wilson   Wilson, Charles Morrow. *Backwoods America.* Chapel Hill: University of North Carolina Press, 1934.

Wyman & Brockway   Wyman, Loraine and Howard Brockway. *Lonesome Tunes: Folk Songs from the Kentucky-Mountains.* New York: H. W. Gray Co., 1916.

War Ballads

Green Willow Tree

A. Abrahams & Foss, p. 79.
   Abrahams & Riddle, p. 143.
   Barry, p. 339.
   Belden, p. 97.
   Brewster, p. 158.
   Bronson, p. 501.
   Brown II, p. 191.
   Brown IV, p. 120.
   Burton & Manning I, p. 37.
   Burton & Manning II, p. 86.
   Bush I, p. 88.
   Cambiaire, p. 93.
   Cazden, p. 46.
   Chappell, p. 43.
   Chase, p. 120.
   Cox, p. 169.
   Creighton (1971), p. 17.
   Creighton & Senior, p. 101.
   Davis (1929), p. 516.
   Davis (1949), p. 35.
   Davis (1960), p. 339.
   Emrich (1974), p. 345.
   Flanders, IV, p. 188.
   Fowke, p. 156.
   Gainer, p. 96.
   Gardner & Chickering, p. 214.
   Greenleaf & Mansfield, p. 43.
   Henry (1938), p. 127.
   Hubbard, p. 43.
   Hudson, p. 125.
   Ives, p. 42.
   Jameson, p. 52.
   Jones (1984), p. 196.
   Leach, p. 669.
   Leisy, p. 128.
   Lomax, A., p. 191.
   McGill, p. 97.
   Moore & Moore, p. 134.
   Morris, p. 326.
   Munch, p. 75.

Niles I, p. 28.
Palmer, p. 108.
Parler, p. 24.
Peters, p. 108.
Pound, p. 24.
Raine, p. 121.
Randolph I, p. 177.
Randolph III, I, p. 195.
Randolph & Cohen, p. 56.
Roberts (1978), p. 89.
Rosenberg, p. 122.
Scarborough (1937), p. 184.
Scott, p. 138.
Sharp, I, p. 282.
Shellans, p. 62.
Shoemaker (1923), p. 126.
Shoemaker (1931), p. 132, 299.
Smith & Rufty, p. 59.
Warner, p. 266.
Wells, p. 53.
Wyman & Brockway, p. 72.

B. Cansler, Loman. "Boyhood Songs of My Grandfather," *Southern Folklore Quarterly* (1954), 18: 177–189, 180.

Colcord, Joanna C. *Songs of American Sailormen.* New York: Oak Publications, Inc., 1964; reissue of a work originally published in 1938, p. 150.

Hugill, Stan. *Shanties from the Seven Seas: Shipboard Work-Songs and Songs Used as Work-Songs From the Great Days of Sail.* London: Routledge & Kegan Paul, 1966, p. 62.

Richardson, Ethel Park and Sigmund Spaeth. *American Mountain Songs.* New York: Greenberg Publisher, 1955; reissue of a work originally published in 1927, p. 28.

C. Almanac Singers	General Electric GE-5016
The Carter Family	ARC PE-7-12-63
	Conqueror 8644
	Vocalion/Okeh 03160
	Columbia 20333
Richard Dyer-Bennet	Keynote KE-517
Pete Seeger	Commodore 3006
Welby Toomey	Challenge 232

D. Horton Barker	*Traditional Singer.* Folkways FA 2362.
	Virginia Traditions: Ballads From British Tradition. BRI-002.
Justus Begley	*Anglo-American Ballads.* Library of Congress L 7.
Bill Cameron	*Child Ballads II.* Caedmon TC 1146.
The Carter Family	*Country Sounds of the Original Carter Family.* Harmony HL-7422.
Warde Ford	*Wolf River Songs.* Folkways FM 4001.

Woody Guthrie	*Woody Guthrie Sings Folk Songs. Vol. 1.* Stinson SLP 44.
Ollie Jacobs	*Child Ballads Traditional in the United States II.* Library of Congress. AFS L 58.
Joe Kelly	*Folk Songs of Ontario.* Folkways FM 4005.
Bascom Lamar Lunsford	*Minstrel of the Appalachians.* Riverside RLP 12-645.
Ewan MacColl and Peggy Seeger	*Marching Songs of the British Isles and America.* Riverside LP 12-637.
Jimmy Morris	*Child Ballads Traditional in the United States II.* Library of Congress. AFS L 58.
The Phipps Family	*The Phipps Family.* Folkways FA 2375.
Almeda Riddle	*Folk Songs From the Ozarks.* Prestige/International 25006.
Jean Ritchie	*British Traditional Ballads in the Southern Mountains.* Folkways FA 2301.
Peggy Seeger	*A Song For You and Me.* Prestige PR 13058.
Joseph Able Trivett	*Joseph Able Trivett.* Folk-Legacy FSA 2.

James Bird

A. Brown II, p. 525.
Brown IV, p. 272.
Belden, p. 296.
Burt, p. 183.
Cox, p. 261.
Hubbard, p. 287.
Peters, p. 228.
Pound, p. 93.
Thompson, p. 3.
Thompson & Cutting, p. 125.
Warner, p. 78.

B. Galbreath, Charles B. "The Battle of Lake Erie in Ballad and History," *Ohio Archaeological and Historical Publications* (1911), 20: 415-456.
King, Mary Elizabeth. "More Light on the Ballad of 'James Bird'," *New York Folklore Quarterly* (1951), 7: 142–144.
McCarthy, Charles A. "James Bird: the Man and the Ballad," *Keystone Folklore Quarterly* (1961), 6: 3–13.
Swetnam, George. "An Early Notice of the James Bird Ballad," *Keystone Folklore Quarterly* (1961), 6: 13–17.

D. Vivian Richman   *Vivian Richman Sings.* Folkways FG 3568.

B. Boswell, George W. "Otherwise Unknown or Rare Ballads from the Tennessee Archives," *Tennessee Folklore Society Bulletin* (1978), 44: 170–178, 172.

Texas Rangers

A. Abrahams & Riddle, p. 14.
　Belden, p. 336.
　Brown II, p. 544.
　Brown IV, p. 276.
　Burton & Manning II, p. 23
　Cohen & Seeger, p. 150.
　Cox, p. 262.
　Fuson, p. 191.
　Henry (1938), p. 350.
　Hubbard, p. 291.
　Lingenfelter, p. 266.
　Lomax, A., p. 331.
　Lomax & Lomax, p. 359.
　Moore & Moore, p. 312.
　Morris, p. 29.
　Ohrlin, p. 129.
　Pound, p. 163.
　Randolph III, II, p. 169.
　Sharp, II, p. 253.

B. Belden, Henry M. "Balladry in America," *Journal of American Folklore* (1912), 25: 1–23, 14.
　Brunvand, Jan Harold. "Folk Song Studies in Idaho," *Western Folklore* (1965), 24: 231–248, 238.
　Goldstein, Kenneth S. " 'The Texas Rangers' in Aberdeenshire," in *A Good Tale and A Bonnie Tune,* ed Mody C. Boatright et al., pp. 188–198.

C. Cartwright Brothers · · · · · · · · · · · · · · · · · · · Victor 40198
　 · Bluebird 5355
　 · Montgomery Ward MW 4460
　Harry "Haywire Mac" McClintock · · · · · · · · · · · Victor 21487
　 · Montgomery Ward MW 4784
　Lester McFarland and Robert A. Gardner Brunswick 168
　 · Vocalion 5177
　Bob and Ruby Ricker · · · · · · · · · · · · · · · · · · · Melotone 6-12-66
　Ernest V. Stoneman · Okeh 45054

D. Cartwright Brothers	*Authentic Cowboys and Their Western Folksongs.* RCA Victor LPV-522.
Paul Clayton	*Cumberland Mountain Folksongs.* Folkways FA 2007.
Leo Gooley	*Ontario Ballads and Folksongs.* Prestige International INT 25014.
Sara Grey	*Sara Grey.* Folk-Legacy FSI 38.
Sloan Matthews	*Cowboy Songs, Ballads and Cattle Calls from Texas.* Library of Congress L 28.
New Lost City Ramblers	*New Lost City Ramblers, Volume 2.* Folkways FA 2397.
Hermes Nye	*Ballads of the Civil War.* Folkways FA 2188.
Joan O'Bryant	*American Ballads and Folksongs.* Folkways FA 2338.

Ballads of Crime and Criminals

The Ballad of the Braswell Boys

B. Hudelston, Jesse, " 'The Ballad of the Braswell Boys': A Putnam County Incident," *Tennessee Folklore Society Bulletin* 46:1 (March, 1980), 25–30.

D. Jesse Hudelston   *Tennessee: the Folk Heritage Volume 2, The Mountains.* Tennessee Folklore Society TFS-103.

Behind the Great Wall

A. Randolph III, p. 151.

C. The Carter Family   ARC 6-03-51
Conqueror 8633

D. The Carter Family   *Country Sounds of the Original Carter Family.* Harmony HL-7422.

Charles Guiteau

A. Arnold, p. 113.
   Belden, p. 412.
   Brown II, p. 572.
   Brown IV, p. 288.
   Burt, p. 226.
   Hubbard, p. 252.
   Hudson, p. 238.
   Lomax, A., p. 273.
   Morris, p. 72.
   Owens (1950), p. 118.
   Pound, p. 146.
   Randolph III, II, p. 29.

B. Bradley, F. W. "Charles Guiteau," *Southern Folklore Quarterly* (December, 1960), 24: 282–283.

C. Kelly Harrell   Victor 20797
   Wilmer Watts and the Lonely Eagles   Paramount 3232

D. Loman Cansler   *Missouri Folksongs.* Folkways FH5324.
   Kelly Harrell   *Anthology of American Folk Music. Volume I. Ballads.* Folkways FA 2951.
                          The Complete Kelly Harrell. Bear Family 12510.
   Clorine Lawson   *I Kind of Believe It's a Gift: Field Recordings of Traditional Music from Southcentral Kentucky.* Meriweather 1001–2.
   Bascom Lamar Lunsford *Songs and Ballads of American History and of the Assassination of Presidents.* Library of Congress AFS L29.
   Phipps Family   *The Phipps Family.* Folkways FA 2325.

Jesse James

A. Abrahams & Foss, p. 130.
   Brown II, p. 561.
   Cohen, p. 107
   Burt, p. 192.
   Fife & Fife, p. 259.
   Henry (1938), p. 320.
   Hudson, p. 235.
   Randolph III, II, p. 18.

B. Henry, Mellinger E. "More Songs from the Southern Highlands," *Journal of American Folklore* (1931), 44: 61–115, p. 87.

McNeil, W. K. "Ballads About Jesse James: Some Comments," *Mid-America Folklore* (1980), 2: 44–51.

D. Although there are numerous recordings of "Jesse James" they all seem to be of different James ballads than this one.

Stagalee

A. Leach, p. 765.
Leisy, p. 306.
Scarborough (1925), p. 92.
Seeger, p. 51.

B. Buehler, Richard E. "Stacker Lee: a Partial Investigation into the Historicity of a Negro Murder Ballad," *Keystone Folklore Quarterly* (1967), 12: 187–191.

Spaeth, Sigmund. *Weep Some More, My Lady.* Garden City, New York: Doubleday, Page, 1927, p. 132.

Wheeler, Mary. *Steamboatin' Days: Folk Songs of the River Packet Era.* Baton Rouge: Louisiana State University Press, 1944, p. 101.

C. Woody Guthrie — Asch-347
Mississippi John Hurt — Okeh 8654
Frank Hutchison — Okeh 45106
Furry Lewis — Brunswick BR-1024
Vocalion 1132
David Miller — Champion 15334
Herwin 75561
Ma Rainey — Paramount 2376
Sam Ku West Harmony Boys — Victor 21422

D. Ed Haley — *Parkersburg Landing.* Rounder 1010.
Sol Hoopii — *Master of the Hawaiian Guitar.* Rounder 1024.
Mississippi John Hurt — *The Immortal.* Vanguard VSD-79248.
Frank Hutchison — *Anthology of American Folk Music. Volume One. Ballads.* Folkways FA 2951.
Professor Longhair — *Live On the Queen Mary.* Harvest SW-11790.
Lloyd Price — *His Big Hits.* Pickwick SPC3518.
The ABC Collection. ABC AC-30006.
Pete Seeger — *American Favorite Ballads, Vol. 2.* Folkways FA 2321.

Charming Beauty Bright

A. Belden, p. 164.
   Brewster, p. 196.
   Chappell, p. 130.
   Cox, p. 342.
   Eddy, p. 113.
   Fuson, p. 136.
   Morris, p. 343.
   Owens (1950), p. 87.
   Randolph III, I, p. 346.
   Scarborough (1937), p. 311.
   Sharp, II, p. 103.
   Sturgis & Hughes, p. 22.

D. Pearl Jacobs Borusky   *Folk Music From Wisconsin.* Library of
                          Congress AFS L55.
     Ollie Gilbert   *Aunt Ollie Gilbert Sings Old Folksongs To Her
                          Friends.* Rackensack RLP495.

The Drowsy Sleeper

A. Belden, p. 120.
   Brewster, p. 170.
   Brown, II, p. 255.
   Brown IV, p. 147.
   Burton & Manning II, p. 91.
   Bush I, p. 60.
   Bush II, p. 63.
   Cazden, p. 3.
   Chappell, p. 81.
   Cox, p. 348.
   Davis (1949), p. 56.
   Eddy, p. 92.
   Gardner & Chickering, p. 86.
   Greenleaf & Mansfield, p. 55.
   Henry (1938), p. 190.
   Hudson, p. 161.
   Jones (1984), p. 210.
   Joyner, p. 53.
   Leach, p. 728.
   MacKenzie (1928), p. 99.

Moore & Moore, p. 196.
Morris, p. 362.
Raim & Dunson, p. 86.
Randolph III, I, p. 244.
Ritchie (1955), p. 219.
Rosenberg, pp. 64, 115.
Scarborough (1937), p. 139.
Sharp, I, p. 358.
Sturgis & Hughes, p. 30.

B. Baskervill, C. R. "English Songs on the Night Visit," *Publications of the Modern Language Association* (1921), 36: 565–614.
   Carter, Isabel Gordon. "Songs and Ballads from Tennessee and North Carolina," *Journal of American Folklore* (1933), 46: 22–50, 32.
   Coffin, Tristram P. "The Problem of Ballad-Story Variation and Eugene Haun's 'The Drowsy Sleeper'," *Southern Folklore Quarterly* (1950, 14: 87–96.

C. Blue Sky Boys — Bluebird B-7661
Montgomery
Ward
MW 7468

Callahan Brothers — Romeo 5353
Oriole 8353
Perfect 13017
Melotone 13071
Banner 33103

Carter Family — Decca 5612
Montgomery
Ward
MW 8071
Melotone 45275

Tiny Dodson's Circle-B Boys — Decca 5386
Kelly Harrell — Victor 20280
Oaks Family — Victor 23795
B. F. Shelton — Victor 40107

D. Joan Baez — *Joan Baez.* Vanguard VRS 9078/VSD2077
Blue Sky Boys — *The Blue Sky Boys.* Camden CAL 797.
— — *The Sunny Side of Life.* Rounder 1006.
— — *20 Country Classics.* Camden ADL2-0726.
The Carter Family — *The Carter Family on Border Radio.* JEMF 101.
Dillard Chandler — *Old Love Songs and Ballads From the Big Laurel, North Carolina.* Folkways FA2309.
Lester Coffee — *Folk Music From Wisconsin.* Library of Congress. AFS L55.

The Country Gentlemen Hazel Dickens and Alice Foster	*The Young Fisherwoman.* Rebel SLP-1494. *Who's That Knocking.* Verve/Folkways FV 9005.
John Duffy and The Country Gentlemen	*Hootenanny.* Design DLP 613.
Ian and Sylvia	*Four Strong Winds.* Vanguard VRS 9133/VSD 2149.
—	*Greatest Hits. Volume 2.* Vanguard VSD 23124.
—	*The Sound of Folk Music, Volume 2.* Vanguard SRV 140.
Louvin Brothers	*Tragic Songs of Life.* Capitol T-769 also issued as Golden Country LP-2201.
J. E. Mainer	*The Legendary J. E. Mainer, Volume 7.* Rural Rhythm RRJEM. 225.
Monroe Presnell	*The Traditional Music of Beech Mountain, North Carolina, Volume 1.* Folk-Legacy FSA 22.
Jean Ritchie	*Singing Family of the Cumberlands.* River- side RLP12-653.
Mike Seeger	*Mike Seeger.* Vanguard VRS 9150/VSD 79150.
B. F. Shelton	*Traditional Country Classics 1927–1929.* Historical HLP8003.
Polly Stewart	*Oldtime Fiddling and Other Folk Music.* Weiser 22866.
Wear Family	*Country and Bluegrass with the Great Wear Family.* Rural Rhythm RR-123.
Harry and Jeanie West	*More Southern Mountain Folk Songs.* Stinson SLP74.
Williams Family	*All In the Family: The Williams Family of Roland, Arkansas.* Arkansas Traditions 004.

I Dreamt Last Night

A. Arnold, p. 62.
   Belden, p. 168.
   Brewster, p. 300.
   Brown II, p. 285.
   Brown IV, p. 157.
   Creighton (1962), p. 54.
   Henry (1938), p. 253.
   Hubbard, p. 137.
   MacColl & Seeger, p. 253.
   Moore & Moore, p. 209.
   Randolph III, I, p. 413.

Sandburg, p. 149.
Sharp, II, p. 17.
Thompson, p. 399.

D. Almeda Riddle *More Ballads and Hymns from the Ozarks.*
Rounder 0083.
— *Songs and Ballads of the Ozarks.* Vanguard
VRS 9158.

Ballads of Lovers' Disguises and Tricks

Little Willie and Mary

A. Barry, p. 24.
Belden, p. 152.
Brewster, p. 356.
Henry (1938), p. 172.
Hudson, p. 153.
Randolph III, I, p. 264.

B. Flanders, Helen Hartness, Elizabeth Flanders Ballard, George Brown, and Phillips
Barry. *The New Green Mountain Songster.* 1939. Reprint, Hatboro, Pennsylvania:
Folklore Associates, 1966, p. 25.
Flanders, Helen Hartness and George Brown. *Vermont Folk-Songs and Ballads.* 1931.
Reprint, Hatboro, Pennsylvania: Folklore Associates, 1968, p. 150.

C. Sam McGee Vocalion 5310

D. Sam McGee *Sam and Kirk McGee From Sunny Tennessee.*
Bear Family 15517.

Miss Mary Belle

A. Belden, p. 150.
Brown II, p. 305.
Brown IV, p. 169.
Burton & Manning I, p. 80.
Burton & Manning II, p. 7, 89.

Cambiaire, p. 64.
Chappell, p. 122.
Cox, p. 316.
Creighton & Senior, p. 134.
Eddy, p. 152.
Gainer, p. 128.
Henry (1938), p. 201.
Hudson, p. 150.
Jones (1980), p. 90.
Jones (1984), p. 202.
MacIntosh, p. 46.
MacKenzie (1928), p. 168.
Moore & Moore, p. 187.
Morris, p. 346.
Owens (1950), p. 91.
Peters, p. 165.
Randolph III, I, p. 258.
Randolph & Cohen, p. 97.
Sandburg, p. 68.
Scarborough (1937), p. 260.
Sharp, II, p. 70.
Wyman & Brockway, p. 88.

B. Rennick, Robert M. "The Pretty Fair Maid in the Garden," *Southern Folklore Quarterly*
   (1959), 27: 229–246.

C. Cousin Emmy
    Brunswick OE 9258
    Decca 24213

D. Judy Domeny — *Calling Me Back.* American Artists AAS-1594.

Cousin Emmy — *The New Lost City Ramblers With Cousin Emmy.* Folkways FTS 31015.

Lola Long — *The Kirkland Recordings.* TFS-106.

Bill Monroe — *Blue Grass Time.* Decca DL 74896.

Obray Ramsey — *Sings Folksongs From the Gateways to the Great Smokies.* Prestige International 13030.

Peggy Seeger and Ewan MacColl — *A Lover's Garland.* Prestige 13061.

The Stanley Brothers — *Country Folk Music Spotlight.* King K-864.

— *1983 Collector's Edition—Vol. I.* Gusto GT-O103.

A. Brown II, p. 306.
   Brown IV, p. 178.
   Cambiaire, p. 95.
   Cox, p. 323.
   Eddy, p. 116.
   Gardner & Chickering, p. 191.
   Hubbard, p. 83.
   MacKenzie (1928), p. 185.
   Randolph III, I, p. 262.
   Ritchie (1955), p. 230.
   Roberts (1978), p. 99.
   Scarborough (1937), p. 268.
   Sharp, II, p. 22.
   Thomas (1931), p. 104.
   Wyman & Brockway, p. 34.

D. Joan Baez   *Joan Baez.* Vanguard VRS-9078.
   Street Butler   *I Kind of Believe It's a Gift: Field Recordings of
                           Traditional Music From Southcentral
                           Kentucky.* Meriweather 1001–2.
   Peggy Seeger   *American Folksongs For Banjo.* Folk-Lyric
                           FL114.

Ballads of Faithful Lovers

Hangman

A. Abrahams & Foss, p. 41.
   Abrahams & Riddle, p. 110.
   Arnold, p. 68.
   Barry, p. 206.
   Belden, p. 66.
   Boette, p. 15.
   Bronson, p. 245.
   Brown II, p. 143.
   Brown IV, p. 76.
   Burton & Manning, p. 85.
   Cambiaire, p. 15.
   Chappell, p. 35.
   Combs & Wilgus, p. 205.
   Cox, p. 115.

Davis (1929), p. 360.
Davis (1949), p. 24.
Davis (1960), p. 221.
Downes & Siegmeister, p. 44.
Eddy, p. 62.
Flanders, III, p. 15.
Fuson, p. 113.
Gainer, p. 64.
Gardner & Chickering, p. 146.
Henry & Matteson, p. 96.
Hudson, p. 111.
Jekyll, p. 58.
Leach, p. 295.
Leisy, p. 153.
Lomax & Lomax, p. 159.
MacIntosh, p. 39.
Morris, p. 295.
Owens (1950), p. 45.
Owens (1983), p. 48.
Parsons (1918), p. 152.
Parsons (1923), p. 189.
Rainey, p. 64.
Randolph III, I, p. 143.
Randolph & Cohen, p. 45.
Ritchie (1955), p. 152.
Roberts (1974), p. 96.
Roberts (1978), p. 61.
Rosenberg, p. 78.
Sandburg, p. 72.
Scarborough (1925), p. 35.
Scarborough (1937), p. 196.
Scott, p. 207.
Sharp, I, p. 208.
Smith, p. 144.
Smith & Rufty, p. 37.
Thomas (1931), p. 164.
Thompson, p. 397.
Warner, p. 268.
Wells, p. 115.
Wyman & Brockway, p. 44.

B. Coffin, Tristram P. "The Golden Ball and the Hangman's Tree," in *Folklore International,*
    ed. D. K. Wilgus. Hatboro, Pennsylvania: Folklore Associates, 1967, pp. 23–28.
Long, Eleanor R. *"The Maid" and "The Hangman."* Berkeley: University of California
    Press, 1962.
Urcia, Ingeborg. "The Gallows and the Golden Ball: An Analysis of 'The Maid Freed
    from the Gallows' (Child 95)," *Journal of American Folklore* (1966), 79: 463–468.

C. Bentley Ball   Columbia A3084
   Lester "Pete" Bivins   Decca 5559

| Charlie Poole | Columbia 15160-D |
| | Columbia 15385-D |

D. Blue Sky Boys — *Presenting the Blue Sky Boys.* JEMF-104.
   Jimmie Driftwood — *The Wilderness Road.* RCA Victor LPM-1994.
   Fred Gerlach — *Twelve-String Guitar.* Folkways FG 3529.
   Harry Jackson — *The Cowboy: His Songs, Ballads, and Brag Talk.* Folkways FH 5723.
   Leadbelly — *Leadbelly: the Library of Congress Recordings.* Elektra EKL-301/2.
   Walter C. Lucas — *Columbia World Library of Folk and Primitive Music. III: English Folk Songs.* Columbia KL-206.
   Charlie Poole — *The Legend of Charlie Poole.* County 516.
   Almeda Riddle — *Badman Ballads.* Prestige/International INT 15009.
   — *Traditional Music at Newport. 1964.* Vanguard VRS-9183.
   Jean Ritchie — *British Traditional Ballads in the Southern Mountains.* Folkways FA 2301.
   — *Field Trip.* Collector Limited Edition 1201.
   Julia Scaddon — *The Folk Songs of Britain. IV.* Caedmon TC-1145B.
   Walker Family — *I Kind of Believe It's a Gift: Field Recordings of Traditional Music from Southcentral Kentucky.* Meriweather 1001–1002.
   The Willis Brothers — *The Willis Brothers (Oklahoma Wranglers).* Masterpiece MLP 204.

John of Hazelgreen

A. Abrahams & Foss, p. 95.
   Barry, p. 369.
   Bronson, p. 512.
   Davis (1929), p. 529.
   Davis (1949), p. 36.
   Davis (1960), p. 350.
   Flanders, IV, p. 281.
   Flanders & Olney, p. 237.
   Moore & Moore, p. 138.
   Morris, p. 330.
   Peacock, II, p. 537.
   Scarborough (1937), p. 225.
   Sharp, I, p. 294.
   Smith & Rufty, p. 62.

B. Barry, Phillips. "Child Ballads and Their Kin," *Bulletin of the Folksong Society of the North-east* (1931), 3: 6-11.
    Zug, Charles G., III. "Scott's 'Jock of Hazeldean': The Re-Creation of a Traditional Ballad," *Journal of American Folklore* (1973), 86: 152–160.

Lord Lovel

A. Arnold, p. 124.
    Barry, p. 139.
    Belden, p. 52.
    Boette, p. 11.
    Brewster, p. 79.
    Bronson, p. 193.
    Brown II, p. 84.
    Brown IV, p. 43.
    Carey, p. 97.
    Chappell, p. 27.
    Cox, p. 78.
    Creighton & Senior, p. 41.
    Cutting, p. 69.
    Davis (1929), p. 240.
    Davis (1949), p. 16.
    Davis (1960), p. 146.
    Eddy, p. 39.
    Flanders, II, p. 148.
    Gainer, p. 45.
    Gardner & Chickering, p. 43.
    Hubbard, p. 17.
    Hudson, p. 90.
    Joyner, p. 41.
    Leach, p. 250.
    Leisy, p. 219.
    Linscott, p. 233.
    Lomax, A., p. 401.
    MacColl & Seeger, p. 70.
    McGill, p. 10.
    Moore & Moore, p. 56.
    Morris, p. 273.
    Palmer, p. 194.
    Peters, p. 202.
    Pound, p. 4.
    Rainey, p. 13.
    Randolph II, p. 193.
    Randolph III, I, p. 112.
    Randolph & Cohen, p. 34.
    Ritchie (1965), p. 22.
    Roberts (1978), p. 43.
    Rosenberg, p. 74.
    Sandburg, p. 70.

Scarborough (1925), p. 55.
Scarborough (1937), p. 99.
Sharp, II, p. 22.
Shoemaker (1923), p. 140.
Shoemaker (1931), p. 146.
Smith, p. 121.
Smith & Rufty, p. 20.
Thomas & Leeder, p. 38.
Thompson, p. 380.
Wells, p. 108.

D. Mark Biggs   *Not Licked Yet.* Centennial CCR-1981.
 Winifred Bundy   *Folk Music From Wisconsin.* Library of
               Congress L 55.
 Alan Lomax   *Texas Folk Songs.* Tradition TLP 1029.
 Peggy Seeger and Guy Carawan *America At Play.* EMI CLP 1174.
 Frank Warner   *Frank Warner Sings American Folk Songs and
               Ballads.* Elektra EKL 3.

Molly Van

A. Brown II, p. 263.
 Brown IV, p. 151.
 Chappell, p. 101.
 Cox, p. 339.
 Eddy, p. 194.
 Gardner & Chickering, p. 66.
 Hudson, p. 145.
 Leach, p. 700.
 Linscott, p. 274.
 Moore & Moore, p. 169.
 Morris, p. 398.
 Pound, p. 78.
 Randolph III, I, p. 254.
 Scarborough (1937), p. 116.
 Sharp, I, p. 328.

D. Bruce Buckley   *Ohio Valley Ballads.* Folkways FA 2025.
 Sara Cleveland   *Ballads and Songs of the Upper Hudson Valley.*
              Folk-Legacy FSA-33.

Seated One Day in a Beautiful Cafe

A. Burton & Manning I, p. 69.

C. Gene Autry   Decca 5501
   George J. Gaskin (cylinder)   Edison 1560
   Jimmie Rodgers   Victor 22319

D. Jimmie Rodgers   *When the Evening Shadows Fall.* RCA Victor
                             LSP-4073(e).

Ballads of Unfaithful Lovers

Barbara Allen

A. Abrahams & Riddle, p. 87.
   Allen, p. 74.
   Arnold, p. 8.
   Barry, p. 195.
   Belden, p. 60.
   Boette, p. 3.
   Botkin, p. 820.
   Brewster, p. 99.
   Bronson, p. 221.
   Brown II, p. 111.
   Brown IV, p. 57.
   Burton & Manning I, pp. 7, 57, 74.
   Burton & Manning II, p. 28.
   Bush I, p. 72.
   Cambiaire, p. 66.
   Carey, p. 98.
   Chappell, p. 32.
   Cox, p. 96.
   Creighton (1962), p. 13.
   Creighton & Senior, p. 49.
   Davis (1929), p. 302.
   Davis (1949), p. 19.
   Davis (1960), p. 182.
   Downes & Siegmeister, p. 34.
   Eddy, p. 52.
   Emrich (1972), p. 572.
   Fauset, p. 113.
   Flanders, II, p. 246.
   Flanders & Olney, p. 197.
   Fowke, p. 100.
   Fowke & Johnston, p. 20.
   Fuson, p. 47.

Gainer, p. 57.
Gardner & Chickering, p. 50.
Greenleaf & Mansfield, p. 26.
Heart, p. 247.
Henry (1934), p. 248.
Henry (1938), p. 82.
Henry & Matteson, p. 12.
Hubbard, p. 20.
Hudson, p. 95.
Ives, p. 50.
Jameson, p. 48.
Joyner, p. 45.
Kennedy, p. 155.
Killion & Waller, p. 255.
Leach, p. 277.
Leisy, p. 22.
Linscott, p. 163.
Lomax, A., p. 183.
Lomax, J., p. 243.
MacColl & Seeger, p. 75.
MacKenzie (1919), p. 100.
MacKenzie (1928), p. 35.
McGill, p. 40.
Moore & Moore, p. 68.
Morris, p. 283.
Munch, p. 88.
Neely, p. 137.
Niles I, p. 18.
Niles II, p. 6.
Owens (1950), p. 49.
Owens (1983), p. 61.
Palmer, p. 82.
Peacock, III, p. 652.
Pound, p. 7.
Raine, p. 115.
Rainey, p. 27.
Randolph I, p. 183.
Randolph III, I, p. 126.
Randolph & Cohen, p. 41.
Rayburn, p. 232.
Ritchie (1955), p. 184.
Ritchie (1965), p. 79.
Roberts (1974), p. 95.
Roberts (1978), p. 52.
Rosenberg, p. 9.
Sandburg, p. 57.
Scarborough (1925), p. 59.
Scarborough (1937), p. 83.
Seeger, p. 79.
Sharp, I, p. 191.
Shoemaker (1923), p. 122.
Shoemaker (1931), p. 127.

Smith, p. 129.
Smith & Rufty, p. 30.
Sulzer, p. 16.
Thomas (1931), p. 94.
Thomas & Leeder, p. 6.
Thompson, p. 377.
Thompson & Cutting, p. 7.
Warner, pp. 128, 425.
Wells, p. 113.
Wheeler, p. 39.
Wilson, p. 99.
Wyman & Brockway, p. 1.

B. Cartwright, Christine A. "Barbara Allen": Love and Death in an Anglo-American Narrative Folksong," in *Narrative Folksong: New Directions,* ed. Carl L. Edwards and Kathleen E. B. Manley, pp. 240–265.

Cray, Ed. " 'Barbara Allen': Cheap Print and Reprint," in *Folklore International,* ed. D. K. Wilgus, pp. 41–50.

Flanagan, John T. "An Early American Printing of 'Barbara Allen,' " *New York Folklore Quarterly* (March, 1964), 20: 1, 47–54.

Flanders, Helen Hartness. " 'Blue Mountain Lake' " and " 'Barbara Allen,' " *New York Folklore Quarterly* (March, 1946), 2: 1, 52–58.

Hendren, Joseph W. "Bonny Barbara Allen," in *Folk Travelers.* ed. Mody B. Boatright *et al.,* pp. 47–74.

Yates, Norris W. "Folksongs in the *Spirit of the Times." Southern Folklore Quarterly* (December, 1962), 26: 326–334.

C.	
Al Craver (Pseudonym for Marion Try Slaughter)	Columbia 15126-D
Vernon Dalhart (Pseudonym for Marion Try Slaughter)	Brunswick 117
	Gennett 6136
Doc Hopkins	Broadway 8307
Bradley Kincaid	Conqueror 7982
	Supertone 9211
	Vocalion VO 2685
Jim New (Pseudonym for Newton Gaines)	Victor V-40253
Maxine Sullivan	Period RL1909
The Vagabonds	Bluebird B-5300

D.	
Ted Ashlaw	*Adirondack Woods Singer.* Philo 1022
Thomas Baynes	*The Lark in the Morning. Songs and Dances from the Irish Countryside.* Tradition TLP 1004.
The Bray Brothers	*Prairie Bluegrass.* Rounder 0053.
Hylo Brown	*Bluegrass Goes To College.* Starday SLP 204.
James B. Cornett	*Mountain Music of Kentucky.* Folkways FA 2317.
Elizàbeth Cronin	*Field Trip. Collector Limited Edition 1201.*
De Danann	*De Danann.* Shanachie 79001.

Rose Day	*Jean Thomas. The Traipsin' Woman.* Folkways FA 2358.
Molly Galbraith	*Folksongs of Saskatchewan.* Folkways FE 4312.
Roscoe Holcomb	*High Lonesome Sound.* Folkways FA 2368.
The Lilly Brothers	*The Lilly Brothers and Don Stover.* Folkways FA 2433.
Sarah Makem	*As I Roved Out. Field Trip—Ireland.* Folkways FW 8872.
Charlie Moore and Bill Napier	*Hootenanny.* King 862.
Glen Neaves and the Virginia Mountain Boys	*Glen Neaves and the Virginia Mountain Boys.* Folkways FS 3830.
Bill Nicholson	*Anglo-American Songs and Ballads.* Library of Congress AAFS L14.
Captain Pearl R. Nye	*The Ballad Hunter.* Library of Congress AAFS L51.
Mr. Rew	*Field Trip—England.* Folkways FW 8871.
Jean Ritchie	*British Traditional Ballads (Child Ballads) in the Southern Mountains.* Folkways FA 2302
—	*Songs From Kentucky.* Westminster WN6037.
Pete Seeger	*American Ballads.* Folkways FA 2319.
Lucy Stewart	*Traditional Singer from Aberdeenshire, Scotland. Vol. 1—Child Ballads.* Folkways FG 3519.
Rebecca Tarwater	*Anglo-American Ballads.* Library of Congress AAFS L1.
Dan Tate	*Virginia Traditions: Ballads From British Tradition.* BRI-002.
George Tucker	*George Tucker.* Rounder 0064.
Various	*Child Ballads, I. Folk Songs of Britain, Volume IV.* Caedmon TC 1145.
Various	*Versions and Variants of "Barbara Allen."* Library of Congress AAFS L54.
Jim Wilson	*Four Sussex Singers.* Collector JEB 7.

The Broken-Hearted Boy

A. Belden, p. 199.
  Brown II, p. 378.
  Brown IV, P. 213.
  Cambiaire, p. 47.
  Cohen & Seeger, p. 74.
  Cox, p. 300.
  Creighton (1971), p. 106.
  Grover, p. 41.
  Henry (1938), p. 354.
  Lomax & Lomax, p. 187.

MacColl & Seeger, p. 219.
Moore & Moore, p. 202.
Munch, p. 85.
Ord, p. 45.
Rainey, p. 38.
Randolph III, I, p. 285.
Randolph & Cohen, p. 101.
Rosenberg, p. 87.
Sharp, II, p. 62.
Thorp, p. 134.
Wyman & Brockway, p. 76.

B. Perrow, Eber C. "Songs and Rhymes from the South," *Journal of American Folklore* (April–June, 1915) 28: pp. 129–190, p. 161.

C. Jules Verne Allen   Victor 23757
   G. B. Grayson & Henry Whitter   Victor V-40324
   Buell Kazee   Brunswick 156-A
   Frankie Marvin   Victor V-40233
   Dick Reinhart   Brunswick 386

D. Jules Verne Allen   *The Texas Cowboy.* Folk Variety FV 12502
   Clarence Ashley   *Old Time Music at Clarence Ashley's Vol. 1.*
                             Folkways FA 2355.
   Delsie Hicks   *Tennessee: The Folk Heritage, Vol. 2. The Moun-
                             tains.* Tennessee Folklore Society TFS-
                             103.
   Pleaz Mobley   *Anglo-American Songs and Ballads.* Library
                             of Congress AFS L12.
   Ashley Moore   *The Kirkland Recordings.* Tennessee Folklore
                             Society TFS-106.
   Melvin Wrinkle   *Music of the Ozarks.* National Geographic
                             Society 703.

The Fatal Wedding

A. Belden, p. 141.
   Brown II, p. 629.
   Brown IV, p. 303.
   Davis (1949), p. 71.
   Greenleaf & Mansfield, p. 368.
   Hudson, p. 195.
   Neely, p. 163.
   Pound, p. 140.

Randolph III, IV, p. 277.
Spaeth, p. 172.

C. Bradley Kincaid

Gennett 6363
Champion 15248
Challenge 366
Silvertone 5186
Silvertone 8217
Supertone 9211
Bell 1178
Melotone
   M12315
Vocalion 02684
Conqueror 7982
Australian Regal
Zonophone
   622215

Red Headed Fiddlers   Brunswick 460
Ernest V. Stoneman   Oriole 946
Edison 52026
Okeh 45084

D. Bob Blair   *Not Far From Here: Traditional Tales and Songs*
Recorded in the Arkansas Ozarks.
Arkansas Traditions (no number).

Bradley Kincaid   *Mountain Ballads and Old-Time Songs.* Old
Homestead OHCS-107

Red Headed Fiddlers   *Texas Farewell: Texas Fiddlers 1922–1930.*
County 517.

The Maiden's Lament

A. Leisy, p. 174.
Seeger, p. 29.

C. The Carter Family

Bluebird B-8350
Montgomery
   Ward M-7356

D. The Carter Family   *In Texas, Vol. 4.* Old Homestead OHCS 1117.
—   *More Golden Gems.* Camden CAS-2554(e).
Bill Harrell   *Ballads and Bluegrass.* Adelphi AD 2013.
Patsy Montana   *A Dutch Treat American Country Style.* Stoof
MU7458.

The Phipps Family
Pete Seeger
—

The Phipps Family. Folkways FA2375.
Frontier Ballads, vol. 2. Folkways FA2176.
Pete Seeger and Rev. Gary Davis at Carnegie Hall. Folkways FN2512.

I'll Hang My Harp On A Willow Tree

A. Heart, p. 278.

B. Pound, Louise. *Folk Songs of Nebraska and the Central West. A Syllabus.* Lincoln: Nebraska Academy of Science, 1915, p. 14.

Jack and Joe

A. Abrahams & Foss, p. 67.
   Brown II, p. 635.
   Brown IV, p. 307.
   Henry (1934), p. 135.
   Henry (1938), p. 173.
   Hubbard, p. 100.
   Morris, p. 64.
   Neely, p. 244.
   Randolph III, IV, p. 336.
   Roberts (1978), p. 206.

C. Blue Ridge Mountain Singers   Columbia 15580-D
   Roy Harvey and the North Carolina Ramblers   Broadway 8080
   Bradley Kincaid   Supertone 9350
                                                       Brunswick 403

   Asa Martin   Conqueror 7745
   McDonald Brothers   Vocalion 5406
   David Miller   Challenge 392
   Riley Puckett   Columbia 15139-D
   Ernest V. Stoneman   Okeh 40408

D. Bradley Kincaid   *Mountain Ballads and Old Time Songs Album Number Four.* Bluebonnet BL 112.
   —   *Mountain Ballads and Old Time Songs.* Old Homestead OHCS 107.
   —   *Old Time Songs and Hymns. Vol. 4.* Old Homestead OHCS-317.

David Miller   *West Virginia Hills.* Old Homestead OHCS-
141.

Betty and Mark Waldron   *Parlor Picking.* Outlet STLP-1028.

Little Massie Grove

A. Barry, p. 150.
  Belden, p. 57.
  Bronson, p. 210.
  Brown II, p. 101.
  Brown IV, p. 53.
  Cambiaire, p. 50.
  Chappell, p. 29.
  Combs & Wilgus, p. 204.
  Cox, p. 94.
  Creighton (1962), p. 11.
  Creighton & Senior, p. 43.
  Davis (1929), p. 289.
  Davis (1949), p. 19.
  Davis (1960), p. 170.
  Eddy, p. 48.
  Flanders, II, p. 195.
  Flanders & Olney, p. 86.
  Fuson, p. 52.
  Gainer, p. 53.
  Gardner & Chickering, p. 46.
  Henry (1934), p. 65.
  Henry (1938), p. 73.
  Leach, p. 269.
  Lomax, A., p. 316.
  MacKenzie (1928), p. 27.
  Manny & Wilson, p. 204.
  Moore & Moore, p. 64.
  Palmer, p. 94.
  Peacock, II, p. 613.
  Randolph III, I, p. 124.
  Ritchie (1955), p. 135.
  Ritchie (1965), p. 36.
  Roberts (1974), p. 92.
  Rosenberg, p. 71.
  Scarborough (1937), p. 143.
  Sharp, I, p. 161.
  Smith, p. 125.
  Smith & Rufty, p. 26.
  Warner, p. 200.
  Wells, p. 110.
  Wyman & Brockway, p. 22.

B. Campbell, Marie. "A Study of Twenty-Five Variants of 'Little Musgrave and Lady Barnard' in Ballad Collections of North America," *Tennessee Folklore Society Bulletin* (1955), 21: 14–19.
   Hand, Wayland D. "Two Child Ballads in the West," *Western Folklore* (1959), 18: 42–45.

C. John Jacob Niles   Victor VM824.

D. Dillard Chandler   *Old Love Songs and Ballads From the Big Laurel, North Carolina.* Folkways FA 2309.

   Paul Clayton   *Folksongs and Ballads of Virginia.* Folkways FA 2110.

   Ruby Bowman Plemmons   *Virginia Traditions: Ballads From British Tradition.* BRI-002.

   Jean Ritchie   *British Traditional Ballads in the Southern Mountains, Vol. 1.* Folkways FA 2301

   Peggy Seeger & Ewan MacColl   *Two Way Trip.* Folkways FW 8755.
   Joseph Able Trivett   *Joseph Able Trivett.* Folk-Legacy FSA-2.

Little Rosewood Casket

A. Arnold, p. 67.
   Belden, p. 220.
   Burton & Manning I, p. 22.
   Davis (1949), p. 121.
   Henry (1934), p. 182.
   Henry & Matteson, p. 32.
   Jones (1980), p. 140.
   MacIntosh, p. 67.
   Neely, p. 230.
   Owens (1950), p. 181.
   Rainey, p. 53.
   Randolph III, IV, p. 269.
   Randolph & Cohen, p. 507.
   Roberts (1978), p. 202.
   Rosenberg, p. 72.
   Shellans, p. 40.
   Stout, p. 83.
   Thomas (1931), p. 100.

C. Vernon Dalhart   Victor 19770.
   Cal Davenport and His Gang   Vocalion 5371.
   Harkreader and Moore   Broadway 8056

Bradley Kincaid	Gennett 6989
	Supertone 9403
	Brunswick 5895
Louisiana Lou	Bluebird 5485
Frank Luther, Zora Layman, and Leonard Stokes	Decca DE-25
John Jacob Niles	Victor VM-824
George Reneau	Vocalion 14997
Ernest Thompson	Columbia 216-D

D. Janette Carter — *Howdayado!* Traditional JC573.
Vernon Dalhart — *Old Time Songs 1925–1930.* Davis Unlimited DU 33030.
Bradley Kincaid — *Favorite Old Time Songs. Vol. 2.* Old Homestead OHCS 155.
Ray and Ina Patterson — *Old Time Ballads and Hymns.* County 708.
Betty Smith — *Songs Traditionally Sung in North Carolina.* Folk-Legacy FSA-53.

Lonesome Scenes of Winter

A. Belden, p. 195.
Brown II, p. 302.
Brown IV, p. 168.
Browne, p. 47.
Creighton & Senior, p. 209.
Henry (1938), p. 298.
Wyman & Brockway, p. 94.

B. Dugaw, Diane. " 'Dreams of the Past': A Collection of Ozark Songs and Tunes," *Mid-America Folklore (1983),* 11: 1–79, 32.
Kittredge, George Lyman. "Ballads and Rhymes From Kentucky," *Journal of American Folklore* (1907), 20: 251–277, 273.

C. Carter Family — Victor 23761

D. Cousin Emmy — *The New Lost City Ramblers with Cousin Emmy.* Folkways FTS 31015.

A. Belden, p. 207.
   Brewster, p. 246.
   Brown II, p. 266.
   Brown IV, p. 152.
   Bush I, p. 62.
   Cox, p. 437.
   Eddy, p. 209.
   Gainer, p. 133.
   Henry (1938), p. 372.
   Hubbard, p. 212.
   Joyner, p. 51.
   MacKenzie (1928), p. 164.
   Morris, p. 397.
   Munch, p. 102.
   Neely, p. 149.
   Owens (1950), p. 75.
   Parler, p. 57.
   Peters, p. 216.
   Pound, p. 81.
   Randolph III, I, p. 311.
   Randolph & Cohen, p. 107.
   Rosenberg, p. 80.
   Sandburg, p. 466.
   Scarborough (1937), p. 335.
   Shoemaker (1931), p. 114.
   Stout, p. 28.
   Sturgis & Hughes, p. 36.
   Williams, p. 312.

C. Blue Sky Boys   Montgomery
                                                          Ward MW 8667
                                                        Bluebird B-8446

D. Blue Sky Boys   *A Treasury of Rare Song Gems From the Past.*
                                             Pine Mountain PMR 305.

   —   *20 Country Classics.* RCA Camden ADL2-
                                             0726.

   Louvin Brothers   *Tragic Songs of Life.* Golden Country LP-
                                             2201.

   Betty & Mark Waldron   *Parlour Picking.* Outlet STLP-1028.
   Mac Wiseman   *New Traditions, vol. 2.* Vetco LP509.

A. Browne, p. 258.
   Wheeler, p. 56.

B. Cothran, Kay L. "Songs, Games, and Memories of Mr. George W. Mitchell," *Tennessee Folklore Society Bulletin* (1968), 34: 63–84, 71.

C. Gene Autry   Champion 45071
   The Carter Family   Montgomery Ward MW
                                                           8003
   Kelly Harrell   Victor 20657
   Earl Johnson & His Dixie Entertainers   Okeh 45194
   Buell Kazee   Vocalion 5221
   Doc Roberts   Supertone 9252
   Connie Sides   Columbia 15009-D
   Ernest V. Stoneman   Okeh 45048
                                                       Pathe 32380

D. The Carter Family   *The Carter Family.* CMH 112.

Three Lovers

A. Abrahams & Foss, p. 46.
   Abrahams & Riddle, p. 181.
   Arnold, p. 108.
   Barry, p. 128.
   Belden, p. 37.
   Brewster, p. 58.
   Bronson, p. 181.
   Brown II, p. 69.
   Brown IV, p. 30.
   Burton & Manning I, p. 25.
   Bush II, p. 96.
   Cambiaire, pp. 34, 115.
   Carey, p. 95.
   Chappell, p. 23.
   Creighton & Senior, p. 40.
   Cutting, p. 65.
   Davis (1929), p. 191.
   Davis (1949), p. 13.
   Davis (1960), p. 123.
   Eddy, p. 29.
   Emrich (1974), p. 281.
   Flanders, II, p. 89.

Fuson, p. 49.
Gainer, p. 39.
Gardner & Chickering, p. 37.
Greenleaf & Mansfield, p. 18.
Henry (1934), p. 41.
Henry (1938), p. 60.
Henry & Matteson, p. 16.
Hubbard, p. 16.
Hudson, p. 78.
Ives, p. 55.
Joyner, p. 35.
Leach, p. 239.
MacKenzie (1919), p. 97.
MacKenzie (1928), p. 20.
McGill, p. 28.
Moore & Moore, p. 51.
Morris, p. 265.
Neely, p. 136.
Owens (1950), p. 39.
Owens (1983), p. 18.
Palmer, p. 79.
Peacock, II, p. 617.
Pound, p. 27.
Raim & Dunson, p. 64.
Raine, p. 112.
Rainey, p. 41.
Randolph III, I, p. 93.
Randolph & Cohen, p. 31.
Ritchie (1955), p. 18.
Ritchie (1965), p. 66.
Roberts (1978), p. 37.
Sandburg, p. 157.
Scarborough (1937), p. 105.
Shoemaker (1923), p. 155.
Shoemaker (1931), p. 160.
Smith, p. 109.
Smith & Rufty, p. 17.
Stout, p. 5.
Thomas (1931), p. 88.
Warner, p. 323.
Wells, p. 106.
Wyman & Brockway, p. 14.

B. Beard, Anne. " 'Lord Thomas' in America," *Southern Folklore Quarterly* (1955), 19: 257–261.
Harris, Richard. " 'Lord Thomas and Fair Ellinor': A Preliminary Study of the Ballad," *Midwest Folklore* (1955), 5: 79–94.

C. Bradley Kincaid
Supertone 9212
Silvertone 8221

D. Horton Barker	*Anglo-American Ballads.* Library of Congress L 7.
Jean Ritchie	*British Traditional Ballads Sung in the Southern Mountains.* Folkways FA 2301.
Mike Seeger	*Folk Music of the Newport Folk Festival 1959–1960.* Folkways FA 2432.
Peggy and Mike Seeger	*American Folk Songs Sung by the Seegers.* Folkways FA 2005.
Hedy West	*Hedy West.* Vanguard VRS-9124.

Pretty Polly

A. Brown II, p. 238.
   Brown IV, p. 137.
   Burton & Manning II, pp. 2, 67.
   Cox, p. 308.
   Creighton & Senior, p. 117.
   Fuson, p. 69.
   Henry (1934), p. 53.
   Jones (1980), p. 93.
   Leach, p. 699.
   Owens (1983), p. 40.
   Randolph III, II, p. 112.
   Roberts (1974), p. 102.
   Roberts (1978), p. 108.
   Scarborough (1937), p. 128.
   Sharp, I, p. 321.
   Wyman & Brockway, p. 79.

B. "Pretty Polly," *Journal of American Folklore* (1899), 12: 248–249.
   Wilgus, D. K. "A Tension of Essences in Murdered-Sweetheart Ballads," in *The Ballad Image: Essays Presented to Bertrand Harris Bronson,* edited by James Porter. Los Angeles: Center for the Study of Comparative Folklore & Mythology, 1983, pp. 241–256.

C. Dock Boggs	Brunswick 132
Coon Creek Girls	Perfect 16–102
	Vocalion 04659
Cranford and Thompson	Melotone 45092
Woody Guthrie	Asch 347
John Hammond	Challenge 168
John Jacob Niles	Victor MV824
The Stanley Brothers	Columbia 20770
B. F. Shelton	Victor 35838
Pete Steele	Archive of American Folk Song AAFS 1702A

D. E. C. Ball and Pete Steele	*Anglo-American Ballads.* Library of Congress L 1.
The Boys From Indiana	*Bluegrass Music Is Out of Sight.* King Bluegrass KB-539.
Coon Creek Girls	*Ballads and Songs.* Old Timey LP-102.
Otis Pierce	*Every Bush and Tree.* Bay 102.
Reno and Smiley	*Hootenanny.* King 862.
B. F. Shelton	*Old-Time Ballads From the Southern Mountains.* County 522.

Ballads of Cowboys and Pioneers

The Disappointed Lover

A. Allen, p. 72.
   Cox, p. 358.
   Fife & Fife, p. 179.
   Larkin, p. 49.
   Lingenfelter, p. 394.
   Lomax, J., p. 51.
   Lomax & Lomax, p. 52.
   Moore & Moore, p. 285.
   Ohrlin, p. 148.
   Sandburg, p. 285.

B. Fife, Austin E. " 'The Trail to Mexico,' " *Mid-South Folklore* (Winter, 1973) 1: 85–102.
   Hendren, Joseph W. "An English Source of 'The Trail to Mexico'," *Tennessee Folklore Society Bulletin* (September–December, 1938) 2: 270–279.

C. Jules Verne Allen	Victor 23757
Harry "Mac" McClintock	Victor 40016
	Montgomery Ward MW 4469
Len Nash and His Country Boys	Brunswick 354
	Supertone 2069
Carl T. Sprague	Victor 20067
	Montgomery Ward MW 4468
Texas Rangers	Decca 5183
Westerners	Conqueror 8205

D. Bill Bender	*Traditional Songs of the Old West.* Stinson SLP37.
Blue Sky Boys	*Folk Music in America: Songs of Local History and Events.* Library of Congress. LBC 12.
Slim Critchlow	*The Crooked Trail To Holbrook.* Arhoolie 5007.
Woodrow Wilson "Woody" Guthrie	*The Ballad Hunter: Parts III & IV.* Library of Congress. AFS L 50.
Charles Ingenthron	*Songs of the Mormons and Songs of the West.* Library of Congress. AFS L 30.
Peter LaFarge	*Peter LaFarge Sings of the Cowboys.* Folkways FA 2533.
Frank Luther	*Git Along Little Dogies.* Decca DL 5035.
—	*Songs and Stories About America.* Vocalion 73738.
Nevada Slim (Pseudonym for Dallas Turner)	*Songs of the Wild West, 2.* Rural Rhythm RRNS163.
Foy Willing	Outlaw CSR 4.

Indian Song

A. Burt p. 142.
   Burton & Manning I, p. 14.
   Hubbard, p. 293.
   Lomax & Lomax, p. 344.
   Randolph III, II, p. 216.
   Scott, p. 179.

C. Marc Williams   Decca 5011.

D. Alec Moore	*The Ballad Hunter. Parts I and II.* Library of Congress AFS L 49.
New Lost City Ramblers	*Remembrance of Things to Come.* Verve/Folkways FTS-3018.

John Henry

A. Boette, p. 55
   Botkin, p. 230.
   Botkin (1949), p. 748.
   Brown II, p. 623.
   Brown IV, p. 298.
   Burton & Manning I, p. 48.

Burton & Manning II, p. 27.
Bush I, p. 53.
Chappell, p. 179.
Cohen, N., p. 61.
Combs & Wilgus, p. 164.
Cox, p. 175.
Davis (1949), p. 294.
Downes & Siegmeister, p. 270.
Emrich (1974), p. 657.
Gainer, p.112.
Henry (1938), p. 446.
Leach, p. 756.
Leisy, p. 189.
Morris, p. 182.
Roberts (1978), p. 160.
Rosenberg, p. 62.
Sandburg, p. 24.
Seeger, p. 82.
White, p. 189.

B. Chappell, Louis W. *John Henry: A Folk-Lore Study.* Jena, Germany: Walter Biedermann, 1933.

Fishwick, Marshall. "Uncle Remus vs. John Henry: Folk Tension," *Western Folklore* (1961), 20: 77–85.

Green, Archie. "John Henry Depicted," *John Edwards Memorial Foundation Quarterly* (1978), 14: 126–143.

Johnson, Guy B. *John Henry: Tracking Down a Negro Legend.* Chapel Hill, North Carolina: University of North Carolina Press, 1929.

C. Bill Bailey   Mercury 70080
   Deford Bailey   Victor 23336
                                                        Victor 23831
   Bailey Brothers   Rich-R-Tone 449
   Birmingham Jug Band   Okeh 8895
   Callahan Brothers   Decca 5998
   Fiddlin' John Carson   Okeh 7004
   Richard Dyer-Bennet   Asch 4613
   Tennessee Ernie Ford   Capitol 3421
   William Francis and Richard Sowell   Vocalion 1090
   Fruit Jar Guzzlers   Paramount 3121
                                                        Broadway 8199
   Sid Harkreader and Grady Moore   Paramount 3023
                                                        Broadway 8114
   Salty Holmes   Decca 24963
                                                        Decca 46116
   Doc Hopkins   Radio 1411
   Mississippi John Hurt   Okeh 8692
   Burl Ives   Columbia 38733
   Earl Johnson and His Dixie Entertainers   Okeh 45101
   Walter "Furry" Lewis   Vocalion 1474

Black Bottom McPhail	Vocalion 04220
Mainer's Mountaineers	Bluebird B-6629
	Montgomery Ward MW 7008
	King 550
New Orlean's Blue Nine	Grey Gull 1263
	Paramount 12003
John Jacob Niles	Victor 2051
Riley Puckett	Columbia 15163-D
Paul Robeson	Columbia 17381-D
Shelton Brothers and Curly Fox	Decca 5173
Spencer Trio	Decca 1873
Ernest V. Stoneman	Edison 51869
Gid Tanner & His Skillet Lickers	Columbia 15142-D
Gid Tanner & Riley Puckett	Columbia 15019-D
Henry Thomas	Vocalion 1094
Hank Thompson	Capitol 2553
Welby Toomey	Gennett 6005
	Silvertone 8146
	Silvertone 5002
	Challenge 228
	Herwin 75332
	Supertone 9245
	Champion 15198
Two Poor Boys	Perfect 181
	Romeo 5080
	Oriole 8080
	Conqueror 7876
Williamson Brothers and Curry	Okeh 45127

D. Rich Amerson	*Negro Folk Music of Alabama: Rich Amerson, Vol. 1.* Folkways FE 4471.
Pink Anderson	*American Street Songs.* Riverside RLP 12–611.
Chet Atkins	*Hum and Strum Along with Chet Atkins.* RCA Victor LSP-2025.
Chet Atkins and Jerry Reed	*In Concert.* RCA Victor CPL2-1014.
Etta Baker	*Instrumental Music of the Southern Appalachians.* Tradition TLP 1007.
James "Iron Head" Baker	*The Ballad Hunter. Parts IX & X.* Library of Congresss L 53
Kenny Baker and Josh Graves	*Bucktime!* Puritan 5005
Harry Belafonte	*Belafonte at Carnegie Hall.* RCA Victor LPC/LSO-6006.
Blue Haze Folk Band	*The Blue Haze Folk Band.* Ranwood 8132.
Blue Ridge Partners	*Mountain Folks.* GHP901.
Dock Boggs	*Dock Boggs, Vol. 2.* Folkways FA 2392.
Bray Brothers and Red Cravens	*Prairie Bluegrass.* Rounder 0053.
Marty Brill	*The Roving Balladeer.* Mercury MG 20178.
Big Bill Broonzy	*Folk Blues.* Emarcy MG 26034
	Folksongs and Blues with Pete Seeger and Big Bill Broonzy. Folkways FS 3864.

	Sings Folk Songs. Folkways FA 2328.
	Portraits in Blues, Vol. 2. Storyville SLP 154.
	Feelin' Low Down. Crescendo GNPS 10004.
	Lonesome Road Blues. Crescendo GNPS 10009.
Fleming Brown	*Fleming Brown.* Folk-Legacy FSI-4.
Hylo Brown	*Hylo Brown.* Rural Rhythm RR 176.
Bruce Buckley	*Ohio Valley Ballads.* Folkways FA 2025.
James Campbell and His Nashville Street Band	*Blind James Campbell.* Arhoolie F 1015.
Johnny Cash	*Blood, Sweat and Tears.* Columbia CL 1930/CS-8370.
John Cephas	*Virginia Traditions: Non-Blues Secular Black Music.* BRI-001.
Chicago String Band	*Chicago String Band.* Testament T-2220.
Paul Clayton	*Dulcimer Songs and Solos.* Folkways FG 3571.
Bill Clifton	*Wanderin'.* Hillbilly HRS-001.
Kyle Creed and Fred Cockerham	*Clawhammer Banjo.* County 701.
Crook Brothers	*Opry Old Timers.* Starday SLP 182.
	Country Music Hall of Fame, Vol. 2. Starday SLP 190.
Jean Davis	*Old Traditions.* Traditional 5117.
Hazel Dickens and Alice Foster	*Won't You Come and Sing For Me?* Folkways FTS 31034.
Dave Dudley	*Songs About the Working Man.* Mercury MG 20899/SR 60899.
Sam Eskin	*Songs of All Times.* Cook 1020.
John Fahey	*Blind Joe Death.* Takoma C 1002.
Lester Flatt, Earl Scruggs and the Foggy Mountain Boys	*Foggy Mountain Banjo.* Columbia CL 1564/CS 8364.
Jesse Fuller	*San Francisco Bay Blues.* Good Time Jazz 12051/S10051.
Doc Hopkins	*Doc Hopkins.* Birch 1945.
Frank Hovington	*Lonesome Road Blues.* Rounder 2017.
Peg Leg Howell	*The Legendary Peg Leg Howell.* Testament T-2204.
Max Hunter	*Max Hunter of Springfield. Missouri.* Folk-Legacy FSA-ll.
Mississippi John Hurt	*Folksongs and Blues.* Piedmont PLP 13157.
John Jackson	*Blues and Country Dance Tunes From Virginia.* Arhoolie 1025.
Henry Johnson	*The Union County Flash.* Trix 3304.
Grandpa Jones	*Grandpa Live.* Monument SLP 18138.
Buell Kazee	*Buell Kazee Sings and Plays.* Folkways FS 3810.
Lilly Brothers	*Lilly Brothers and Don Stover.* County 729.
Alan Lomax	*Texas Folksongs.* Tradition TLP 1029.
Bascom Lamar Lunsford	*Minstrel of the Appalachians.* Riverside RLP 12-645.
Charlie McCoy	*Good Time Charlie's Got the Blues.* Monument KZ 32215.

Fred McDowell	*When I Lay My Burden Down.* Biograph BLP 12017.
	Long Way From Home. Milestone 93003.
	Live In New York. Oblivion OD 1.
Uncle Dave Macon	*At Home.* Davis Unlimited DU-TFS 101.
Maggie Valley Boys	*Maggie Valley Boys.* Rural Rhythm RR 170.
Memphis Slim	*Broken Soul Blues.* United Artists UAL 3137/UAS 6137.
Paul Vernon and Wade Miles	*Dance Music: Breakdowns & Waltzes.* Library of Congress LBC 3.
Bill Monroe	*Bill Monroe Sings Country Songs.* Vocalion VL 3702/73702.
Charlie Moore	*Charlie Moore Sings Good Bluegrass.* Vetco 3011.
Mountain Ramblers	*Blue Ridge Mountain Music.* Atlantic SD-1347.
Bashful Brother Oswald	*Banjo & Dobro.* Tennessee NR 4990.
Peg Leg Sam	*The Last Medicine Show.* Flyright LP 507–508.
George Pegram	*Galax Old Fiddlers' Convention.* Folkways FA 2435.
Pinetop Slim	*Anthology of the Blues: Blues From the Deep South.* Kent KST 9004.
Larry Richardson, Red Barker, & the Blue Ridge Boys	*Larry Richardson, Red Barker, & the Blue Ridge Boys.* County 702.
Carl Sandburg	*Carl Sandburg Sings His American Songbag.* Caedmon TC 2025.
Mike Seeger	*Tipple, Loom & Rail.* Folkways FH 5273.
Jimmie Skinner	*Country Singer.* Decca DL 4132.
Kilby Snow	*Mountain Music Played on the Autoharp.* Folkways FA 2365.
I. D. Stamper	*Red Wing.* June Appal 010.
Stoneman Family	*Old-Time Tunes of the South.* Folkways FA 2315.
Stringbean	*A Salute to Uncle Dave Macon.* Starday SLP 215.
Jimmie Tarlton	*Steel Guitar Rag.* Testament T-3302.
Merle Travis	*The Way They Were Back When.* Shasta LP 517
	Guitar Player. Shasta 523.
Uncle Josh and Hoss Linneman	*That Dobro Sound's Goin' 'round.* Starday SLP 340.
Howard Wallace	*Old-Time 5-String Banjo.* Jewel LPS 186.
Doc Watson	*On Stage.* Vanguard VSD 9/10.
Connie Williams	*Blind Connie Williams.* Testament T-2225.
Martin Young and Corbett Grigsby	*Mountain Music of Kentucky.* Folkways FA 2317.

A. Abrahams & Foss, p. 128.
   Allen, p. 96.
   Fife & Fife, p. 217.
   Hudson, p. 224.
   Larkin, p. 115.
   Lingenfelter, p. 436.
   Lomax & Lomax, p. 125.
   Moore & Moore, p. 325.
   Ohrlin, p. 153.
   Owens (1983), p. 98.
   Randolph III, II, p. 239.

B. Silber, Irwin and Earl Robinson. *Songs of the Great American West.* New York: Macmillan, 1967, p. 197.
   Sires, Ina. *Songs of the Open Range.* Boston: C. C. Birchard & Co., 1928, p. 6.
   Tinsley, Jim Bob. *He Was Singin' This Song.* Orlando: University Presses of Florida, 1981, p. 92.

C. Charles Baker — Champion 45052
   Cartwright Brothers — Columbia 15410
   Carl T. Sprague — Victor 21194
   Frank Wheeler and Monroe Lamb — Victor 40169 / Montgomery Ward MW 4470
   Marc Williams — Brunswick 304

D. Cecil Gill — *The Yodeling Country Boy.* Bluebonnet BL 101
   Van Holyoak — *Cowboy Songs, II.* Arizona Friends of Folklore AFF 33-2.
   Harry Jackson — *The Cowboy.* Folkways FH 5723.
   Lucy Johnson — *Music of the Ozarks.* National Geographic Society 703.
   Harry McClintock — *Harry K. McClintock: "Haywire Mac."* Folkways FD 5272.
   Nevada Slim — *Songs of the Wild West, II.* Rural Rhythm RRNS 163.
   Marty Robbins — *Gunfighter Ballads.* Columbia CS 8158.
   Carl Sprague — *Authentic Cowboys and Their Western Folksongs.* RCA Victor LPV-522.

A. Brown II, p. 619.
   Fife & Fife, p. 241.
   Larkin, p. 144.
   Lomax & Lomax, p. 124.
   Ohrlin, p. 159.
   Randolph III, II, p. 204.

C. Asa Martin   Oriole 8213
   Arthur Miles   Victor 40156
   Charles Nabell   Okeh 40252
   Pat Patterson and Lois Dexter   Banner 32091

D. Dave Fredrickson   *Songs of the West.* Folkways FH 5259.

Young Alban and Amandy

A. Barry, p. 36.
   Hubbard, p. 98.
   Morris, p. 128.
   Randolph III, IV, p. 118.

B. Peabody, Charles. "Texas Version of 'The White Captive,' " *Journal of American Folklore*
   (1912), 25: 169–170.

The Young Man Who Wouldn't Hoe Corn

A. Belden, p. 440.
   Botkin, p. 874.
   Brewster, p. 307.
   Eddy, p. 243.
   Moore & Moore, p. 386.
   Owens (1950), p. 219.
   Randolph III, III, p. 195.
   Seeger, p. 42.

B. Dugaw, Dianne. " 'Dreams of the Past': A Collection of Ozark Songs and Tunes," *Mid-America Folklore* (1983), 11: 1–79, 57.
   Lumpkin, Ben Gray. "Four Folksongs from Kemper County," *Mississippi Folklore Register* (1967), 1: 20–24, 20.

C. Buster Carter and Preston Young   Columbia 15702-D

D. Buster Carter and Preston Young

Anthology of American Folk Music. Volume One. Ballads. Folkways FA 2951.

Pete Seeger

Frontier Ballads. Vol. 2. Folkways FA 2176.

The Williams Family

All In the Family. Arkansas Traditions 004.

PROPERTY OF
HIGH POINT PUBLIC LIBRARY
HIGH POINT, NORTH CAROLINA

Indexes

Index of Titles

Index of Locations

ALABAMA
Gadsden   102
Livingston   66
Mobile   56
Point Clear   110

ARKANSAS
Bee Branch   164
Bethel Grove   144
Canaan Mountain   127
Fox   157
Marshall   78, 106
Pine Top   154
Spring Valley   34, 160
Springdale   53
Woolsey   38

FLORIDA
Gainesville   130
Perry   146

GEORGIA
Thomaston   135

KENTUCKY
Ary   140
Barren County   88
Elkton   82
Nobob   58

MISSISSIPPI
Hamburg   113
Louisville   123, 124

NORTH CAROLINA
Crossnore   116
Ebenezer   75, 86
Hendersonville   80

SOUTH CAROLINA
Murrell's Inlet   72, 132

TENNESSEE
Cookeville   48
Knoxville   148
Morrison City   98
Nashville   42
St. Bethlehem   93

VIRGINIA
Bowling Green   150
Brown's Cove   44, 60, 70, 91
Fancy Gap   74, 96, 137
Meadows of Dan   119

Index of Informants

About the Editor

A native of North Carolina, W. K. McNeil is the folklorist at the Ozark Folk Center in Mountain View, Arkansas. He earned an M.A. from the Cooperstown Graduate Program at the State University of New York, and a Ph.D. in Folklore from Indiana University. Author of many studies on American folklore and editor of two other anthologies, *The Charm is Broken* and *Ghost Stories from the American South,* McNeil is also the general editor of the American Folklore Series.

PROPERTY OF
HIGH POINT PUBLIC LIBRARY
HIGH POINT, NORTH CAROLINA